A
Soldier's Search
for Meaning

Camp Gruber–Dachau–Vienna

By
James F. Dorris
and
JC Howell MD

A Soldier's Search for Meaning, published January, 2020
Editorial and proofreading services: Kathleen A. Tracy; Karen Grennan
Interior layout and cover design: Howard Johnson
Cover artwork: *Enigma* by Gustave Doré, part of his *Souvenirs of 1870,* after
France's defeat by Prussia in 1870. From Wikimedia Commons

 **SDP Publishing**

Published by SDP Publishing, an imprint of SDP Publishing Solutions, LLC.

To obtain permission(s) to use material from this work, please submit a written
request to:

SDP Publishing
Permissions Department
PO Box 26, East Bridgewater, MA 02333
or email your request to info@SDPPublishing.com.

ISBN-13 (hardcover): 978-1-7338214-6-9
ISBN-13 (paperback): 978-1-7338214-7-6
ISBN-13 (e-book): 978-1-7338214-8-3

Library of Congress Control Number: 2019919099

Copyright 2020, James F. Dorris and JC Howell MD

Printed in the United States of America

In memory of
Lieutenant Daniel Preston McLaurin
who made this book possible.

Kathleen Tracy's incisive observations, suggestions, and edits elevated this manuscript. A special thank you goes to Karen Grennan for proofreading services.

OVERTURE

*He who has a **why** to live for can bear almost any how.*

— Nietzsche

How does one find a **why,** a **purpose** or **meaning**?

Existentialists claimed there is no grand purpose of life, no meaning in the universe beyond what meaning we give it.

Human beings can't find a grand meaning of life because it doesn't exist, and absurdly, they can't live without meaning.

— Camus

One must find and fulfill their own meaning. Meaning doesn't satisfy unless it's personal. Meaning differs from human to human. Life asks different questions of each of us.

— Viktor Frankl

Viktor Frankl wrote *Man's Search For Meaning* based on his experiences and personal search as an inmate in four concentration camps, including Auschwitz. A human's search for meaning, he observed, is the primary motivation in their life. *This meaning is unique and specific in that it must and can be fulfilled by one alone—only then does it achieve a significance which will satisfy one's own will for meaning*—one's true essence meaning.

In order to find meaning, Frankl also observed that one must have and maintain internal freedom, which in a concentration camp, war, or life requires decisions, moment by moment, minute by minute, and hour by hour that nurture

7

inner freedom. The alternative is to submit to the forces commanding one's attention, losing one's very self, surrendering freedom insidiously, then losing human dignity, and becoming a typical inmate, or in a broader context a slave of an institutional world, living in despair.

What about the liberating soldier, the institutional being with a name, rank, and serial number, trained for war? Can a soldier find true essence meaning?

Before addressing this question, we must explicate the prerequisite for human meaning; i.e., what is internal freedom and what decisions nurture it? At Auschwitz Frankl recognized that the degrees of internal freedom of an inmate were proportional to the richness of their life experiences, including intellectual, sentient, and spiritual experiences—and the deeper these experiences were the greater options and refuge they provided for one's attention, helping one to avoid becoming a slave who gave up choice, gave up freedom, and submitted to the SS, Capo, and other forces driving their attention. The ability to freely self-direct attention toward the riches of one's life experiences underpins internal freedom.

Human beings experience the world as their attention reconstitutes in each now, now, etc., in either language-thinking frames or sensory frames, in either pre-reflective or reflective consciousness, in the data spheres of sensate, of language, and of their value world. I experience the blue ocean as a pre-reflective experience in real time at the beach. I sit in a room and direct my attention to visit images of the blue ocean in my reflective consciousness. Swimming, I experience the cool blue water in my sensate sphere. I direct my attention to think with words to describe the enormous blue ocean in my language sphere. I visit why I like clean blue water in my value-world sphere.

What happens to attention when one faces starvation and threat of death while forced to dig sixteen hours a day, day after day? What happens to attention when one has to focus on killing an enemy and face the threat of being captured, wounded, or killed, day after day? What happens to one's rich life experiences?

Attention comes in two varieties: bare attention as in aware of things, and selective attention as in focused on specific things. Bare attention emerges passively from incoming— external or internal sensory. In the human brain, all sensory is transmitted to the thalamus. There are two thalami, masses of gray matter lying between the two hemispheres of the brain, functioning as a relay station to the cerebral cortex. For example, incoming visual and auditory sensory data arrive at the thalami and stimulate sensory-data spikes which give rise to oscillating brain waves known as Gamma EEG waves, sweeping from the front to the back of the brain or cerebral cortex at 40–100 waves per second. These oscillating brain waves, discovered after the introduction of digital EEG, carry large amounts of data and activate relevant cerebral circuits, producing a preconscious mosaic which generates consciousness and perception, like one's perception of an ink blot where prior encounters with similar blots, mood, and bias color the experience of the phenomenon—where phenomenon means the image or appearance of the blot as it's perceived in the mind during that specific encounter.

For example, a German soldier's sudden arm movement on the horizon of a battlefield produces a bare attention phenomenon in the mind of an observing American soldier lying in a foxhole prepared for battle. The same arm movement by an SS guard on the other side of a concentration camp produces a slightly different phenomenon in the mind of an observing camp prisoner who's digging a mass grave for murdered inmates.

Selective attention allows both the American soldier and the inmate to self-direct attention within consciousness for an immediate and more detailed pre-reflective examination, looking for a weapon near the arm in motion, while the preconscious review continues—the reflective examination of the arm in motion—comparing the arm movement to memories of a similar arm in motion phenomenon, evaluating the potential threat. Bare attention continues bringing in new data during the above, building upon the existing mosaic for the arm-in-motion conscious phenomenon. When no threat is perceived, the American soldier relaxes, and the inmate continues digging.

Selective attention can also free one from the phenomena that bare attention passively produces, e.g., an inmate in a concentration camp marching toward a work site can self-direct his attention away from the dawn's freezing rain and visit an image of his wife in reflection, experiencing her physical beauty and love as he steps oblivious to the mud and ice.

Brain research in the early twenty-first century has demonstrated that attention training, where attention is driven to the same areas of the brain over and over, can change neuron connections, can change neuron production of neurotransmitters, and can change a human's brain—empowering and warning us that who or what controls attention can train and change our brains, gradually, without our consent or awareness.

Moreover, who or what drives attention builds one's repertoire of reflective phenomena, controlling what one can become and eventually changing what one is, burying one's rich life experiences.

What will we become?

It's time to get back to the story question. Can an institutional soldier find true essence meaning? How did Frankl find his meaning? Private James F. Dorris and Viktor E. Frankl had different life experiences. They faced different questions from life, and both struggled to maintain their internal freedom while facing remarkably similar forces vying for control of their attention and freedom. Dorris was an American soldier searching for meaning, fighting to liberate the oppressed, and hoping for a future. Frankl was an inmate of a concentration camp facing death and extermination, struggling to find meaning for himself and others, to live for another day, the future.

The Nazis were masters at demeaning and dehumanizing—masters at training inmates' attention while treating them as animals, taking away their internal freedom. Frankl experienced this firsthand every day. One day a guard threw a rock at him to drive his attention toward digging, treating him like a domestic animal. He wrote *that being treated like a beast that was not even worth punishing had a more painful effect than a beating.* The Nazis controlled his attention through work, insults, beatings, depravity, and the threat of death. If he refused to work, disobeyed a guard or Capo, or failed to respond to an order, he would have been killed immediately.

Dorris experienced attention training in the military and on the battlefield. He experienced the threat of death every day. He had to attack, kill, and conquer a formidable enemy. And if he disobeyed a superior's order on the battlefield, he could've been executed.

In addition, in order to maintain internal freedom, Frankl and Dorris had to refrain from falling under the spell of their own will for power or will for pleasure while they struggled to find meaning. For examples, in the case of Frankl he didn't succumb to addiction to hate thinking, and in Dorris's case he didn't succumb to the power he had over his prisoners and innocent bystanders—the entitlement to do wrong.

They both experienced hunger, starvation in the case of Frankl, thirst, extreme cold, snow, wind, rain, fatigue, sleep deprivation, injuries, pain, sickness, disease, threat of death, loss of those they loved, death and destruction all around them. Every morning brought the unknown. What would life ask of them, and would they be alive for sunset?

They directed their attention to nature, to their duties, to helping others, and to the phenomenology of God (the repertoire of phenomena that played in their minds when they self-directed their attention in thought and prayer toward God). And they directed their attention to reflect on mental images of their loving family members, where they experienced love through reflection. All of the above served as a refuge for their attention, nurturing their internal freedom, keeping them from becoming a typical inmate or typical soldier.

And the greatest and most reliable refuge was where they directed their attention in critical moments. They directed their attention to a reality outside the reach of all human faculties, beyond the world, and toward a central goodness in their phenomenology of God. This vital sanctuary remained unaffected by the world at war.

Richard Dawkins, an ardent atheist and evolutionary biologist, wrote *The God Delusion* ignoring the significance of internal freedom and God in one's search for meaning. He declared that the belief in God has no rational foundation and condemned humans to genetics and natural selection as they search for meaning in an institutional and meaningless world. Dorris and Frankl's experiences undermine Dawkins's thesis, which as proposed would unfold over time like another species of the failed Nazi master-race idea.

Frankl observed firsthand that the predicate for Dawkins's thesis, genetics and natural selection, had had little influence on internal freedom and decision making required to find meaning in death camps. Dorris witnessed that those adopting Dawkins's a priori, a Godless universe, were ill-equipped to endure the atrocities of warfare. After the war he watched as many of his fellow soldiers and commanders, having lost their internal freedom and their very selves insidiously, returned home imprisoned by their horrific memories, the phenomenology of war, and later many of them developed depression, post-traumatic stress disorder, alcoholism, and drug addiction.

Another interesting and important aside, internal

freedom is necessary for the alcoholic or drug addict to get sober one day at a time. First they have to get the alcohol or drug out of their bodies, and then they have to free their attention from the phenomena they created while addicted, which limit their internal freedom and too often lead them to drink and drug again.

How do they stay sober? According to Alcoholics Anonymous founders Bill Wilson and Bob Smith, Step One is admitting the problem, and Steps Two and Three are critical to begin the physical, mental, and spiritual journey to freedom.

Step Two: Came to believe a power greater than ourselves could restore us to sanity.

Step Three: Made a decision to turn our will and our lives over to the care of God as we understood him.

Creating internal freedom by directing their attention toward God allows the abstinent addict or alcoholic the chance to remain sober and to find personal meaning.

Frankl tried to help his fellow inmates, and it was then that he realized that not just any meaning would work for them—the dilemma. Only the pursuit of one's personal meaning provided the drive to overcome *any how* (any obstacles), giving one a purpose and a future that allowed them to endure the concentration camp life. Frankl and Dorris also observed that by finding meaning in suffering, one's suffering became less severe. Lastly, their observations revealed that when inmates and soldiers lost their future meaning, a projected purpose needing to be fulfilled, they gave up and died in camp or were killed in the next battle.

The final question that *A Soldier's Search* answers is the most important question for humankind going forward. As discussed earlier, Frankl observed that the meaning of life was different and specific for each human. He concluded there was no grand purpose of life. Likewise, Albert Camus surmised there was no grand purpose inherent in the universe but that should not stop individuals from creating their own meaning. *We can't find a grand meaning of life, and we can't live without meaning*—the great puzzle. Until now, the grand purpose of life has eluded our awareness because we were too close to our temporal and divergent meanings and because we didn't understand what one is and what we could become if we maintain internal freedom underpinned by the phenomenology of God.

Dorris's story provides the missing piece of the mystery. His journey provides the additional data that Frankl didn't have—a retrospective analysis and forward projection of a liberating soldier's data, regarding one and we. The empirical and logical analysis of Dorris and Frankl's threads of meaning, which converged in Vienna, deliver the concrete grand meaning of life inconceivable until this moment in history.

Imagine the power of the entire human race pursuing a common purpose that transcends time—individuals searching for and fulfilling their personal meaning in the context of a concrete grand purpose of life.

Enjoy Dorris's story.

JC Howell MD

OPERATION
NORDWIND

The gray, twilight sky had faded into freezing darkness about two hours ago—no moon, no stars. At least it wasn't snowing, and for the moment all was calm. It was January 24, 1945, and Europe was experiencing its worst winter in twenty-five years. We were just inside the snow-covered, heavily-wooded Ohlungen Forest, dug in, facing the Haguenau Forest in Northeastern France where elements of the German Army had gathered less than two kilometers away, preparing to attack us.

I, Dorris, James F., serial number 14711824—a six-foot-three, 150-pound, twenty-year-old private in the US Army, wearing two pairs of wool long johns under an olive infantry uniform, field jacket, overcoat, wool socks, calf-high, black leather boots, and wool hat under my helmet—knelt on the icy floor of a foxhole, rubbing my leather gloved hands together, trying to restore feeling in my fingers.

Suddenly, the sky lit up in front and behind us with

rockets and red flares bursting up and down our line. The darkness no longer hid our positions. I stood and gazed past the firebreak in the forest on the right and then got out of the hole, walked over, and peered down the tree line on my left. The red light from the flares reflected off the snow and ground fog as bright as afternoon sunlight. Our entire 222nd Regiment had been deployed, about four thousand troops in foxholes dug into a foot of snow and frozen ground, forming a line about seven-thousand yards long, west to east.

"Get down! Incoming!" yelled Sergeant Lewis from about twenty yards away.

Explosions flashed with yellow-orange bursts across the western horizon, like heat lightning flickers, producing the loudest thunderclaps I'd ever heard. The earth shook, and I hurried back and jumped into our foxhole. The rising and fading high-pitched whistling sounds of incoming artillery played like we were in a war movie. It seemed surreal.

"Shit! Shit-fire! Damn Krauts," said Private Mingus, my ammo man. He flipped his cigarette into the snow and rolled next to me. A large tree branch, riddled with acorn clusters, fell over our hole. I curled into a fetal position and pulled my helmet over my face, noticing my five-week-old beard had frozen, turning into tiny icicles.

The guttural hissing sounds of low-flying rockets played in the foreground, and more artillery shells exploded in the fog a few hundred yards in front, creeping toward our position. About twenty minutes later, the distant screams of wounded soldiers played. The Germans had found their range and were pounding the guys on our left. Moans and cries for assistance filtered through the trees.

"Hold your positions!" Sergeant Lewis yelled, as he ran past us toward the wounded.

My heart pounded, adrenaline rushing through my veins. The fear of death consumed my attention. I stared at Mingus's profile, his stubby beard, lean face, and long nose.

Are we going to die tonight? The meaning of our lives reduced to dying without a fight in this grave we'd spent hours digging.

Closing my eyes, I prayed for peace for my fellow soldiers and for our families back home. Then the thought: *I'm not going to die* played in my mind. *I have a purpose, and this is not it. There's a reason I'm here; Mingus too. Something we have to discover, something we have to fulfill.*

Another round of blasts shook me to my core, covering me with dirt. My heart ached, and tears welled up in my eyes. *I will never see my mother, father, or Albert again.*

I closed my eyes again and visited my family in reflection. Their images were more luminous than the morning sun. I warmed at their love for me and my love for them. And for a long moment, nothing else mattered.

A nearby boom brought me back to reality. I didn't want to let my family down, and I didn't want to let my fellow soldiers down.

"Hail, Mary, full of grace …," I prayed in a low voice, and repeated, raising my voice in desperation as *kabooms* erupted about fifty feet behind us.

Then our mortars and a few 105 mm howitzers countered, silencing the German artillery. I rolled over, looked toward the heavens in gratitude, stretched out my numb legs, and sighed. When the Germans resumed, shaking the earth with wave after wave of explosions, I covered my ringing ears. The last hour had seemed like an eternity. I didn't know how much more I could take.

They can't keep this up forever, I told myself.

Concussion blasts from mortar fire continued one after another from all sides, like roadside bombs shaking my conviction.

God, I know I've not been perfect. If I'm going to die, at least let me die fighting. I don't want to die like this, I prayed, inhaling the strong pine scent from an evergreen cut in half by a low-flying Nebelwerfer rocket.

Their artillery waned then stopped. Mingus and I stood and cleared the downed tree limbs. My ears continued to ring. Somewhat disoriented, I couldn't even remember the names of the towns we were defending. I asked Mingus for my ammo. He dropped to his knees and reached into his backpack. He handed me eight magazines and a few moments later gave me a couple of crackers and cheese. We'd eaten bland canned meat, K-rations, earlier.

"Thanks."

I chewed, savoring the sharp cheddar and salty crackers and remembered the names of the towns—Neubourg and Schweighausen. Mingus said that battalion command suspected elements of three Kraut divisions including a panzer division were on their way to break through our line.

I shook my head in disgust. "Panzers."

Mingus munched on a cracker and added that we wouldn't have our tanks and armored vehicles for at least twelve more hours.

"That's why they're attacking us now," I murmured, not expecting a reply.

He added that he'd heard rumors the Krauts wanted to retake Strasbourg for Hitler's anniversary and then reminded me that the Nazis had come to power on January 29, 1933.

We'd stayed near Strasbourg when we arrived at the front by train about four weeks ago on Christmas. Everything had changed since that day. I hated to think about it. I blocked out what had happened and thought about how beautiful the tall gas lights, garlands, and wreaths were that had decorated the city's main street. I thought about the great, pink sandstone cathedral in Strasbourg serving as a symbol of hope for the proud French people.

The rumors Mingus had heard made sense. The Germans had been attacking the Seventh Army for the last three weeks, pushing toward the famous French city, and had broken through just a few miles north of our present position, forcing the Seventh's retreat. We mostly green replacement troops had been brought up to buy some time as the Seventh Army regrouped, and this morning we'd gotten word that we had to hold the Germans at all costs.

The clouds parted, and a shaft of moonlight broke through.

"We've got to hold 'em."

"Yep," Mingus said, with a sly grin. "A fight to the death so be ready, Dorris."

I'd never killed a human before. A few others in our regiment had seen combat in the Aleutian Islands and had killed Japanese soldiers in hand-to-hand combat. I didn't like to think about killing. I preferred the idea that I would stop them with my .30-caliber bullets.

I turned my eyes from the moonlit treetops of the Haguenau Forest, found Mingus's gleaming brown eyes, and nodded solemnly. I wouldn't let him down.

He pulled out his machete, spat, and shined it on his jacket sleeve. "Yep. We're going to stop 'em or die trying. No surrender and no retreat, that's what Sergeant Ervin said. But don't worry, Dorris. We're going to shut 'em down."

I hoped he was right and watched in silence as he waved his machete like a sword and thrust it upward into the air as if he were impaling the heart of the German Army. Mingus was a little, wiry guy from a family of coal miners in Pennsylvania. He was tough as nails and a fearless soldier. We'd become buddies immediately when we first met at Camp Gruber. He was a gifted fellow with a keen sense of awareness, a country boy with an eighth-grade education, and a savvy poker player with a generous heart. He'd taken me out to celebrate his poker winnings on several occasions. He always seemed to have a winning hand, a positive attitude. And he trusted me as I trusted him. There was no one else in the regiment who I'd rather have by my side tonight. I knew he would give his life for me as I would for him.

Waiting was the worst part, and the longer we waited, the colder it got. I pulled out the magazine loaded in my Browning automatic rifle, blew into the chamber for several seconds, tested the trigger, and reloaded. Relieved the firing mechanism hadn't frozen, I decided I was ready. I had fourteen twenty-round magazines, eight stacked on a blanket to my left and another six snapped on my ammo belt.

The artillery barrage began again; I believed ours and theirs. The ground shook, and shrapnel struck the oak tree in front and then a pine directly behind us. My heart pounded, my hands shuddered, and for a split second, I wished we could run home as fast as possible, all the way back to America.

God help us, I prayed.

A couple of minutes of silence passed. Remembering Lt. Col. Walter Fellenz's words in boot camp—*every battle is your defining moment*—I grew calm and strangely resolved. His words continued to play in my mind. It was as if he'd known one day we'd be thinking about his fateful words.

This is our defining moment. This must be my reason for being.

I was a descendant of the Greek general Josef Dorris who'd fought under Julius Caesar. I had ancestors who'd fought in the American Revolution, the Civil War, and WWI. I was destined to be here, to fight in this battle. *This is my moment.* I closed my eyes and prayed for the strength to do God's will and fulfill my meaning.

A small artillery or mortar round produced a hum and exploded about thirty yards in front of our foxhole. The pink glow from Nazi flares had faded. Sweeping our eyes back and forth anxiously, Mingus and I struggled to see through the swirling, low-lying fog, fearing the Germans had moved out from the cover of the Haguenau forest and were launching grenades at us.

"The Krauts are coming," Mingus whispered, clutching his M-1 rifle, finger on the trigger. "I can feel them marching."

A moment later I knew he was right. "I can hear them,"

I said in a low voice, gazing over the front sight of my rifle into the fog.

Clack-clack.

The distant sounds of tank tracks with creaking rollers approached, crushing small hardwoods and churning through the snow.

"Hold your fire," Sergeant Ervin whispered forcefully, as he ran past our position.

My mind seemed to go into slow motion then. A childhood memory played in my consciousness—I was riding the little green school bus home, staring at the driver's cigarette smoke, dense and swirling like fog in the front of the vehicle.

I **turned and gazed** out the school bus window at the grocery store and bicycle shop. Mr. Mulkey was helping Mrs. Jackson with her groceries. The sign over the bicycle shop read: *42 days till Christmas*. It was the fall of 1931 in Chattanooga, Tennessee.

Mom, Dad, my little baby brother, and I lived in a neighborhood of small family homes, built about five years earlier, on rolling hills thick with trees known as Belvoir. Last Sunday, November 8, I'd celebrated my seventh birthday. I'd only received one present, but that was okay. We were living in a depression, which meant there were few jobs, and most people didn't have any money. My mother thought we were blessed because we had a home, and Dad had a job at Delaney's Iron Casting Foundry.

The bus stopped at the corner of Belvoir Avenue and Brainerd Road. I got off, ran across the green field, an empty lot, through Mr. Kelly's front yard, and then turned down a gravel road. There it was: a little white house—our home. I skipped up the driveway and entered through the back door. I waved at Mother in the kitchen.

"Jimmy, how was school?"

"Good."

I smiled, grabbed a cookie from the cookie jar, and made a beeline to my room. I couldn't wait. I wanted to finish building my miniature log cabin. Kneeling on the hardwood floor, munching on a homemade sugar cookie, I pulled my logs and partially built cabin from under the bed. I took my time and assembled the back wall then part of the roof.

"Jimmy, honey, you should go outside and play with your friends," my mother, Mary Siener Dorris, whispered from the doorway, with a green apron around her blue dress. She'd started cooking dinner. She said that my little brother, Albert, was asleep, taking a nap in his room.

"Aw, Mom. I'm too tired to play. I've been at school all day," I said. "I want to finish building my Lincoln Log cabin, my birthday present."

"Sweetheart, you're going to wake up Albert."

"No, I won't. I promise." As soon as I'd said that, the roof and support logs came crashing down to the floor.

Mother put her finger over her mouth, gazed toward Albert's room, then whispered, "Go outside and play with Billy and Tommy."

Looking at my logs spilled everywhere, I stood and shook my head in frustration. Mother approached and wrapped her arms around my shoulders. I hugged her waist and found her eyes.

"Mom, will Albert ever be able to play with me?"

She crouched, and as she stared into my eyes, tears appeared in her blue eyes. I thought about when I was two years old when she would hold me in the rocking chair, singing, *I will love you always, and I will be thinking of you always.*

"Sweetheart, remember Albert has a mental handicap. He loves you very much, and he will play with you someday. He'll need your special attention and support. I know you'll give him that when the time comes."

"I will," I said, bobbing my head. "*Always.*"

Mom pulled me into a tight embrace and told me that

God had given me a special brother because I was special. With new tears she kissed me and told me to go play.

"Okay. It's okay," I said.

She stood and ushered me to the hall. I shot her a smile and ran out the back screen door into the cool breeze and hurried to the street. Gray clouds had filled the afternoon sky. Bluebirds and robins chirped in Mrs. Thornton's trees, perched on half-naked branches. A gold leaf drifted in the breeze, moving to-and-fro as it fell. Red, brown, and gold leaves had covered our neighbors' yards. I wished I'd put on my jacket. The cold air had made chill bumps on my arms.

"Hey, Dorris, over here," yelled Billy and Tommy Daniels in unison.

I could see them playing in their front yard. I reached the top of the gravel road and stopped. They were always mean to me for some reason. Billy smirked at me then threw a pine cone striking Tommy on the side of his face. I waved reluctantly. They played rough. Billy was two years older than me, and Tommy was one year younger. They were both bigger than me. But I was glad I was faster.

"Over here, Dorris," Tommy yelled, and launched a handful of sweet gum balls toward Billy, now ducking behind the hedges.

"Hey, you guys want to play tag?" I asked.

"That's a girl's game," said Billy. Tommy nodded in agreement. "Come here, Dorris," Billy said, with a grin at Tommy.

I approached Billy cautiously.

"What are you afraid of?" Billy asked.

I looked up at him. "Nothing."

Billy puffed up his chest and approached. When he got close, he lifted his arms as if he was going to push me. I backed up in response. Tommy had snuck up and was on all fours behind me, and I tumbled to the ground and rolled in the leaves.

Tommy grabbed my legs while Billy punched my side, saying, "You're a damn Catholic."

"You damn Catholic," Tommy echoed.

I kicked up my knees, freeing my legs, rolled, got to my feet, and fled toward home. Up the hill and down the road, I ran with tears streaming down my cheeks. I barreled through the back door of our house and into the kitchen where Mother was standing near the stove, stirring a pot.

"Jimmy, Jimmy, what's wrong?" she cried, then knelt and hugged me. "Did you hurt yourself?"

I was crying and couldn't catch my breath.

"Calm down, sweetheart," she whispered, embraced me again, and rubbed my back.

I took a deep breath and told her that Billy and Tommy had tried to beat me up.

"Why would they do that?"

I shook my head. I didn't know why. Mother had me blow my nose into a napkin. "I didn't do anything to them," I said. "Mom, what's a damn Catholic? They called me a damn Catholic."

She pulled me back into her arms, squeezing me tight. "Some people are ignorant and intolerant of others' beliefs. Billy and Tommy just don't understand."

"What?"

"We are Catholic. That's our religion. Jesus gave us our religion."

My mouth gaped. I couldn't believe I was a Catholic. After several moments in Mother's arms, my breathing relaxed. Dad's car pulled into the driveway. Mother released me and asked me to place the plates on the table. I pivoted toward the sink, washed my hands, and picked up three plates from the counter.

Mother had cooked mashed potatoes, gravy, and cornbread. I loved her gravy. Setting the table, my mouth watered at the smell as she singed pork chops in the skillet. My dad came in with a bag of potatoes and set them on the back porch table then welcomed Mother with a kiss and me with a hug.

He said that people were lined up all the way down Eighth Street waiting for a handout of food at Loveman's department store. Mother shook her head, looking sad; Dad shook his head too. Mom told him that she'd given out sandwiches to a homeless couple passing through our neighborhood around lunchtime.

I lowered my head and tried to think of something to say. I told Dad that I'd tried to give to others, but sometimes they were too proud to accept it.

"Joey turned down the peanut butter and jelly sandwich that Mom had made for me to give him today. He said that he wasn't hungry, but I knew he was, so I left the sandwich on the table, hoping he'd get it after I left."

"Good boy, Jimmy," Dad said, drying his hands at the sink. He took his seat at the head of the table. "Dinner smells delicious."

Albert cried, and Mom went to get him. I went over, hugged Dad again, and sat in his lap. He asked if I'd built my log cabin. I told him I almost had the roof on, just a few more logs, but then it collapsed. He rubbed my head and said we'd work on it this weekend.

"We're going fishing this weekend, remember?" I said.

"Yes, we are."

Mom brought Albert, and Dad helped fasten him in the highchair then kissed him on the cheek. Albert had a large cute head and tiny eyes.

"Hey, Albert," I said, and smiled.

"Jimmy, sit down. I want you to say grace," Mom said.

I sat, reached for Dad's hand and Albert's tiny hand, glanced at Mom across from me, and bowed my head. "God, thank you for my mother, my father, and Albert. Bless us O Lord with these thy gifts, which we are about to receive. Amen." I grinned. "Let's dig in."

On an overcast and cool Saturday morning the day before Palm Sunday, during the spring of 1942, Albert and I readied to ride bicycles through our Belvoir neighborhood.

"Jimmy, Jimmy, are you going to fight Tojo?" Albert asked as we walked toward the garage.

"No, I'm not going to fight Tojo."

"Jimmy, don't go fight. Promise me you won't."

"Don't worry. I'm not going to fight. I'm only seventeen."

"Jimmy, don't leave us."

"I won't leave."

I rolled Albert's bike—a red, twenty-five-inch Schwinn—out of the garage to him then got mine, a green, twenty-seven-inch Schwinn. "Let's get riding. Dad wants to go fishing around noon."

"Mom said you might have to fight. I don't want you to fight."

I laid my bike down, walked over, and hugged Albert. "Don't worry. I'm not going away to fight."

"I love you, Jimmy. I love you."

"I love you, Albert. Let's ride."

Albert jumped on his bike, wobbled down the driveway,

and then accelerated down the street in perfect balance. I was always amazed at how well he could ride once he got moving. I caught up with him, and we rode for about an hour, with Albert in the lead, circling around our neighborhood and then in a wider circle through the back alley several times.

Albert stopped suddenly.

Uh oh.

I hit my brake and slid in the gravel, laying my bike down on the curb, striking my knee on the road in the process.

"Damn, it burns!" I cried, holding my right leg.

Albert rushed over. "What happened, Jimmy? Are you okay? Are you okay?"

I sat on the curb, pulled up my jeans, and noticed some road rash and a little blood over my knee cap.

"Jimmy, you're bleeding."

"I'm okay," I said, frustrated with Albert. I had no idea why he'd stopped, and I didn't want to ask. He would think it was his fault that I'd crashed. I hobbled over to my bike and pulled it upright, grimacing in pain.

"Jimmy, Mom says you should give up your pain to the Lord."

I rotated toward Albert and couldn't keep from smiling, even though my leg stung like the dickens. "Yeah, you're right. I'll give up my pain. Let's head home."

Albert jumped on his bike, and I followed. Each pedal stroke became a little easier. Mom was right. I reached the top of the hill and then coasted home.

We hopped off our bikes in the driveway and walked them toward the garage. Mom and Dad were loading our gray-blue Plymouth. Dad placed our fishing poles catty-corner in the back seat with corks and hooks fastened to the poles sticking out the window. Mom placed a picnic basket in the back seat.

"Mom, Jimmy hurt his knee; he's bleeding," said Albert.

I shook my head, saying, "It's just a little scrape." I leaned my bike on the kickstand.

"Let me see," said Mom.

I pulled up my jeans. "It was bleeding, but it stopped."

Mom furrowed her brow. "Come inside."

She led me to the kitchen. I sat at the table while she cleaned my wound with soap and water. My knee burned like it was on fire; I gritted my teeth and held my breath as she put iodine on it. I knew it would hurt. Then it hit me.

"Dang! that stings," I said, squeezing my thigh.

Mom blew on my wound with several quick breaths. It took several long moments for the pain to ease. I sighed, thanked Mom, rolled my pants leg down, and got up slowly. We joined Albert and Dad in the garage.

"Boys, get your jackets," Dad said. "The wind will be whipping across Chickamauga Lake."

Albert ran inside and brought back our red jackets. We both gave Mom a hug and jumped into the car. I rode up front, and Albert sat in the back as we cruised toward our favorite fishing spot. Dad didn't say a lot; he was a man of few words. We turned off the highway onto a gravel road that led to the lake. We parked, unpacked, and hiked in silence toward our favorite spot. The green lake appeared beneath a natural rock wall covered with moss. We followed the trail toward a willow tree near the edge of the lake. Dad found a big rock for the lunch basket while I loaded Albert's and my hook with worms.

Dad grinned at me, grabbed his pole, and threaded a worm over his hook. "All right, boys. Let's catch some big ones."

We settled by the willow tree, dropped our lines in the water, and wedged our poles between stacks of smooth river rocks. The three of us sat in silence watching our corks bobbing over ripples caused by the wind. Albert was especially quiet when he fished.

"Dad," I whispered. "Did that form I made last week for Mr. Jones turn out okay?"

He smiled. "Jimmy, that new lathe has really helped, hasn't it?"

I nodded. "Yeah."

Dad had bought me a new lathe the previous Christmas. I'd been cutting wood forms for the foundry for a couple of years. I'd made quite a bit of money during high school.

"Mr. Jones said that drive wheel fit perfectly on his yarn-spinner."

As I shot my dad a smile, the tip of Albert's pole curled, and he jumped in excitement. Dad moved over to help. Albert waited till his cork submerged then lifted his catch out of the water. The fish flipped several times swinging to-and-fro, scaring Albert, causing him to almost lose his glasses.

He'd caught a large bream. Albert was so happy, and I grinned in joy. Dad patted his shoulder and helped unhook the fish then held it tightly in his hand. Albert stared at the fish for several seconds before Dad threw it back in the lake.

"He was a big one," Dad said. "Half-pound, at least."

Albert glanced at me, smiling. "I got lucky."

I shook my head to disagree. "You're a great fisherman, Albert."

We sat in the cold air for about an hour, waiting to catch another fish. The wind blew right through my jacket. It seemed cold enough to snow. We took a break, huddled around the lunch basket, and ate some delicious tuna sandwiches and corn chips, sipping on warm tea from a thermos and talking about Albert's fish. Neither Dad nor I had gotten even a nibble.

After lunch we fished some more. It turned icy cold. Albert was shivering. Dad suggested we leave and try next week when it should be warmer. We grabbed our poles then hiked back to the car and jumped in to escape a gust of frigid wind. Heading home, Albert was beaming because he'd caught the only fish, and he knew Mom would be so happy and proud of him. I couldn't wait to see the look on her and Albert's faces when he told her.

When Dad turned off Belvoir to our street, I could see Mom walking up the driveway with the mail in her hand. She was staring at a letter, her face serious. She hurried to the back door as we pulled onto the driveway. Something was wrong. We continued into the garage, and I jumped out and ran inside. My mother stood near the kitchen table with tears in her eyes.

"What is it? What's wrong?" I asked.

Her face was twisted in pain. She didn't speak. She handed me the envelope; it was from the United States Army. My heart stopped then pounded as I ripped it open and silently read the letter.

> To James F. Dorris Jr.
>
> Order to report for induction from the president of the United States.
>
> You have been selected for training and service in the United States Army.

I couldn't talk. I couldn't swallow. I could barely breathe. I heard Dad and Albert coming in the back door. Mother's lip quivered as if her heart had been broken.

Tears filled my eyes as I reached out and pulled her tight, managing to whisper, "It's going to be okay. It's going to be okay."

"What is wrong with Mommy? Mommy, why are you crying?" Albert asked, his voice cracking as he cried, and embraced both of us.

CAMP GRUBER

Lying on a bunk bed in Barracks #222, I took a big bite out of one of Mom's homemade sugar cookies, thinking about what to write in a thank-you letter to my family for the birthday package. I'd just finished a twenty-mile march, carrying a thirty-pound backpack and a twenty-one-pound Browning automatic rifle (BAR), and was exhausted. It was Thursday, November 9, 1944.

It was a long story how I'd ended up here at Camp Gruber, Oklahoma. Because I was only seventeen when drafted, I got deferred then got another deferral to finish my first semester of college. I then completed basic training at Fort McClellan in Alabama, performed well on a placement exam, and was sent to engineering school in Fargo, North Dakota. This past summer I'd begun my second boot camp here at Gruber.

After the Normandy invasion every soldier who could fight was needed in Europe. The Forty-Second Infantry Division had been reactivated a year earlier at Gruber under the leadership of General Harry J. Collins, and soldiers from all over the United States had come here to reconstitute the 222nd, 232nd, and the 242nd Regiments—about fifteen thousand soldiers. In 1927 General MacArthur had nicknamed the Forty-Second the Rainbow Division. And we were like a rainbow from one end of the United States to the other; we had men from almost every state.

I'd gone through basic training in Alabama and engineering school in Fargo. And now I was learning how to use a powerful automatic rifle that shot a .30-caliber round with a six-hundred-yard range, sending out a burst of fire like a machine gun, and I could take down a six-by-six-foot concrete wall with two twenty-round magazines at two-hundred yards. I'd also learned to shoot in semi-automatic mode, so I wouldn't draw attention to my powerful weapon unnecessarily.

Sergeant Ervin had trained us to take out snipers, fight hand-to-hand, and the appropriate way to take in surrendering soldiers. Ervin and Lieutenant McLaurin had warned that we'd be holding ground, fighting in foxholes, and advancing against fortified German positions in their own country, their backs against the wall, making our job much more difficult.

We'd become real soldiers over the last two months. We weren't battle-tested, but we trusted our training and commanders, who were serious military leaders. And we were learning how to respond under combat conditions where every moment could mean the difference between life and death and where you had to follow commands. A soldier could be court-martialed and executed for disobeying a legal order in combat. That had been pounded into our thick skulls.

> To Mother, Dad, and Albert,
> I'm sending my love. Thank you for my birthday presents. I'm smiling and munching on a sugar cookie as I write. Several of my buddies have enjoyed Mom's delicious cookies and brownies. My friend Mingus told me to tell Mom thanks.

Albert, you and Dad would love it here. The camp was built a couple of years ago on several hundred acres of farmland with a large lake stocked with bass, bream, and catfish, and the fishing is awesome. And we could ride our bikes on the rolling hills, flat stretches of green fields, and brown prairie grass, which stretches for miles, while chasing after wild horses. It really is beautiful here.

Mother, you would love the facilities. There are over two thousand buildings, a one-thousand-bed hospital, a post office, and lots of shops. We even have a giant movie theater. The railroad comes right into camp, and soldiers are coming and going every day. The barracks are long, two-story buildings painted white with green trim.

The dining halls are gigantic too. They feed us great—beef, chicken, turkey, vitamin-enriched bread, and potatoes—but we burn up calories faster than we can eat. I've never been as hungry as I've been here, especially when we play war games in the field for several days, eating rations and living off the land.

I've met some great men and great soldiers. Gulley, Boraff, and Mingus are my new buddies. We're in the same platoon made up of about thirty other soldiers from all over America—New York, Chicago, Los Angeles, Dallas, etc. They're great guys, all decent and tough.

Lt. Daniel P. McLaurin is the officer in charge of our platoon. He's a Citadel graduate and one of the finest men I've ever met. He's about six-foot-two, fast, strong, and smart. Sergeant Ervin is also in our platoon. He's twenty-nine and looks like that movie star, John Wayne, blond and blue-eyed. He's taller than me, bigger and stronger too. I would not want to have to face him in battle. He's what the guys call a cold-blooded killer.

I'm in Company A, four platoons or about 120 soldiers and part of the First Battalion, which is about one thousand men. You won't believe this, but during war games I broke through enemy lines and captured the battalion commander, Lt. Col. Walter Fellenz. I took his rifle, and he shoved a knife against my stomach, which he had hidden in his sleeve. He told me to never let a prisoner get close to me.

Fellenz is a West Point graduate, and he's one of the smartest military minds I've ever met. He seems to know every soldier under his command and their weaknesses, truly amazing. He's also aware of Captain Bellum, one of the company commanders I don't like. Bellum was a history professor before he got drafted. He's not good, a lazy guy who's caused us to do several twenty-mile marches with backpacks. Fellenz watches everything he does now.

Lt. Col. Fellenz picked me and several others to disrupt the battalion during a war-game event. I came up with the idea to herd a group of about twenty wild horses—led by a white stallion—through camp during the early morning. We did it and were a great success. Lt. Col. Fellenz was pleased. But Mess Sergeant Marcinek didn't like that we disrupted breakfast. Thank God the horses didn't hurt anyone.

I don't know what's next, but I'll tell you as soon as I can. Albert, Mom, and Dad don't worry. I love you all.

Mom, I'm reading the Novena of St. Therese the Little Flower every day. I'm trying to figure out what all this means, learning what I'm supposed to do, hoping I have the strength to do it. I'm praying, and I know you're all praying together every night for me. That gives me such a great feeling, just knowing. You have all my love.

Love, Jimmy

On **November 23, Thanksgiving** Day, our boots thumped on the hard ground as we proceeded in two lines toward a ferry in the shipyard at Hoboken, New Jersey. We'd just finished a noisy, three-day train ride from Gruber, packed in boxcars like cattle going to slaughter.

Gazing toward the black hull of a gigantic ship anchored in the harbor, I marched behind Gulley's bobbing towhead. A gust from the dark-green Hudson River, the gateway to the Atlantic, produced chill bumps on my arms. Unrolling my jacket sleeves, inhaling the salty breeze, I thought: *At least we were free from that stinky, urine-stained train.*

Glancing at all the transport ships in the harbor, I couldn't believe the might of the US military. Boraff directed my eyes toward our transport ship. It looked huge.

"Halt!" Sergeant Ervin said. "At ease."

Coming to an abrupt stop, I almost bumped into Gulley, and Boraff almost bumped into me. A hundred yards ahead to our right, two platoons from the 232nd Regiment drilled.

The sergeant called out, "Sound off!"

"One two," the troops responded.

"Sound off."

"Three four."

"Cadence count."

"One two three four, one-two—three-four."

"The heads are up, and the chests are out. The arms are swinging in cadence count."

"One two three four, one-two—three-four."

"Head and eyes are off the ground, forty inches, cover down ..."

Their voices faded as they marched toward the river. On our left three-dozen pale, youthful faces in olive fatigues engaged in calisthenics on an overgrown baseball field. They jumped and reached for the blue sky, maintaining their formation. They were a platoon from the 242nd Regiment.

Several from my platoon walked across the road to an old, white building to relieve themselves. I followed up the stairs, waited in line, and took my turn in the single bathroom. The commode worked, but the stained porcelain sink didn't. Bounding down the outside stairs onto the landing area, I slowed to a stop when I saw two bullies from the 242nd picking on a young slow soldier, who reminded me of Albert. One of the bullies, a big redhead, threw a knife at his boot. The young soldier pulled the knife out of the plywood and threw it back, piercing the redheaded bully's boot. He screamed and pulled out the knife. The other bully—short, stocky, and bald—lunged toward the young soldier.

Seeing fear in his eyes, I stepped in front of the kid and told the bullies they weren't going to do a damn thing to him. They could see I was ready to pounce, so they both turned, cursing, and headed for the aid station near the train. I told the kid to find his platoon and hang in there. He thanked me, and I wished him well then hurried back to my outfit.

A jeep appeared and sped past us toward our ferry. It was Lt. Col. Fellenz. Gulley poked my ribs with an elbow and asked if I'd found anything to eat. I shook my head no. We waited and waited and finally loaded onto the ferry. I leaned over the rail watching the propellers churning the brackish water like foamy dirty dishwater as we headed for our transport ship.

From my back pocket, I pulled out the Novena in honor of St. Therese, the Little Flower. I read it every day. I'd been through all nine days many times, but it never failed. Every time I read it, I discovered something new. I read *The Second Day* as we slowly made our way across the harbor to our ship. The passage focused my mind on living a contemplative life centered around prayer.

We docked and prepared to board, orderly by platoon. Mingus shouldered his way next to me.

"This old steamboat ain't fit to fish in. Dorris, do you get seasick?"

"I don't know. All I care about right now is getting some grub. I hope the mess deck is open."

We climbed the cable stairs onto the deck. The *Edmund B. Alexander* was huge, at least two-and-a-half football fields long and about thirty yards wide. We stepped inside the main doors of the covered deck.

"Wow, this is going to be great," Gulley said. "Look at this titanic dining hall."

There were too many stained-wood chairs and long mahogany tables to count. Considering the ship was carrying the entire 222nd Regiment, I decided the dining hall area needed to be this massive. About a hundred soldiers were lined up in three cafeteria lines where kitchen staff hustled to-and-fro. The aroma of turkey and dressing wafted from the serving area. My mouth watered.

As I looked around, my gaze followed the perfect mahogany spindle balusters supporting a rail running up the twenty-foot staircase to the balcony above where Col. Henry Luongo, commander of the 222nd, stood talking to Lt. Col. Fellenz and General Henning Linden, commander of the 222nd, 232nd, and 242nd Regiments, named the Linden Task Force. Luongo looked like a professional soldier even in general issue army fatigues, and there was something special about Linden, with his plump face and probing eyes.

He just looked like a general. Fellenz too had serious brilliance behind his large, dark eyes.

Turning my head and rotating toward the authoritative voice of our platoon leader, I stood at attention, found Lt. Daniel P. McLaurin's eyes above Gulley's blond head and saluted.

"Carry on, men. Let's get some grub. It's going to be a long voyage."

I grabbed a tray and got in line behind Mingus. I nodded at Sergeant Marcinek as he stepped through the swinging doors from the kitchen area. I was happy to see his round, pug face. He was a great cook. Waiting in line, I thought about the long journey ahead, wondering if my buddies and I would make it back alive. I bowed my head and prayed in silence for a moment, asking God for our safe return.

Around nine that night, a couple of hours after our turkey and dressing dinner, Gulley, Boraff, Mingus, and I walked on the wet, gray, steel-top deck, gazing beyond the bright red, white, and yellow lights on the transport ship anchored several hundred yards in front of us. The misty rain and fog had reduced the sleepy town of Hoboken to rows of yellow streetlights.

We paused by the guard rail, and I peered directly below. More troops had arrived by ferry. I noticed Captain Bellum, my least favorite company commander, his face riddled with wrinkles. His academic career as a history professor had not prepared him to function as a commander. He was the kind of leader you didn't want to fight for because he only cared about himself. I joined the others as we stood at attention and saluted him.

"At ease, men," Captain Bellum said. He informed us that we weren't leaving the harbor till tomorrow, which was fine by me, and then told us to find our platoon leader.

"Yes, sir," we responded.

We followed Bellum into the dining hall then turned toward our sleeping quarters and passed the ship's library. Boraff recognized one of his old high school mates, Jonesy, a short, black-haired, blue-eyed fellow. Greeting us, Jonesy said that he worked in the engine room as a mechanic and had the grease-stained hands to prove it. We gathered around to hear the latest scuttlebutt. Jonesy said that if we had good weather, it would take a couple of weeks to make the trip. He thought we were going to Marseilles, France, a famous Mediterranean port city.

Jonesy knew a lot about this old ship. The *Edmund B. Alexander* had been built in 1905 as a transatlantic luxury liner based in Hamburg, Germany. It was initially christened the *SS Amerika*, and in 1912 had a brush with infamy when on April 14 one of the ship's officers sent a warning message about icebergs to the Hydrographic Office in Washington, DC. That message was relayed to the Marconi operator on the *Titanic* just a few hours before the liner went down.

The *Amerika* was in Boston when World War I started in Europe. Instead of leaving port as planned, the *Amerika* stayed to avoid getting captured by the Royal Navy. The United States remained neutral for the first three years of fighting before joining the Allies in 1917. At that point the US government seized the *Amerika* and refitted it as a transport ship. She'd carried Rainbow Division troops then too. Jonesy boasted the ship no longer used coal and now used oil as fuel and was capable of 17 knots.

Jonesy suggested we take a look at the ship's library, which had its original stock of books. He admitted the luxury was gone, and in fact the ship had been used recently as a floating barracks for about 1200 men. Last month they'd redone the sleeping areas with canvas hammocks six high to accommodate six thousand troops.

We left Jonesy and headed for the library. I glanced toward the balcony and saw General Linden walking with a general who had two stars on his helmet.

I nudged Boraff. "Who is that?"

Mingus and Gulley turned their heads toward the two generals.

Gulley chuckled, and said, "That, my friends, is the commanding officer of the Forty-Second Infantry Division, Major General 'Hollywood' Harry J. Collins."

"Why do they call him Hollywood?" I asked.

"Have you ever seen a general who acts or dresses more like a Hollywood star?" Gulley replied.

I smiled. "Yeah, I see what you mean."

Hollywood was dressed impeccably: perfectly creased uniform pants and shining black leather boots. Most noticeable was the silver scarf around his neck.

"If you ask me, all officers are Hollywood material," Mingus muttered. "They're no good at fighting."

"I wouldn't say that about Lt. McLaurin," I replied.

"Yeah, you're right, Dorris."

We all agreed McLaurin was different, and we were lucky to have him leading our platoon.

We entered through the old library's double glass doors. Giant fans adorned the high ceiling. Row upon row of bookcases and shelves lined the walls, each filled floor to ceiling with books. Mingus picked up *Ben Hur* by Lew Wallace, and some pages fell out. Gulley picked up *Practical Mysticism* by Evelyn Underhill, and the cover fell apart. I helped put the books back together and placed them on the shelf. We hurried out of the library and headed for our sleeping quarters.

Later after lights out, my hammock rocked back and forth. I barely noticed. It didn't bother me as I lay staring at Mingus sleeping directly above and listening to Boraff snoring directly below. I wondered what it would be like to sleep in these hammocks out on the rough sea. Would we be able to sleep, tossing to-and-fro? I said my prayers and tried turning onto my left side. My shoulder would've jabbed Mingus in the back. So I lay supine in darkness hoping I'd fall asleep.

It **only took three** days on the high seas to realize if I
was tired enough, I could sleep in a swinging hammock.
Now I just needed to shake the nausea and persistent diz-
ziness of my seasickness. Nothing had worked, but I believed
it would go away if I could see land or step on solid ground
for a few minutes. Unfortunately, we were in the middle of
the Atlantic Ocean.

Lying in my hammock, staring at Mingus swinging in
his hammock above me, I decided to try something else. I got
up and visited the deck, hoping that seeing some other transport ships might mitigate my symptoms. Johnson, a tall young
Texan from Dallas, approached. We were the only two on
deck. We talked about seasickness for a moment then stared
at the inky black sea, no other ships in sight.

Johnson pulled a three-inch ivory knife from his jacket, a
good-luck charm that he'd carried every day for ten years. He
smiled, flipping the knife over and under his long fingers—
until it slipped out of his hand and struck the guard rail, rico-
cheting into the sea.

Johnson's face grew pale. "Shit! Shit! That was the best
damn knife I've ever owned. Damnit!"

I shrugged, not knowing what to say, aware my seasickness had disappeared. I thought the loss of his knife was an

omen. We needed to hold tightly the things that we cherished. Our lives could be lost in an instant on the battlefield, or worse things could happen if we were taken prisoner.

"Dang, that knife shot out of your hand like a bullet," I said.

He lowered his head, turned, and walked away, not understanding my reference. I'd wanted to say more about the loss of his knife. I wanted to warn him. Leaning with my elbows on the rail, looking out at the horizon's first pink light of dawn, I prayed for my fellow soldiers and asked God for the strength to perform all of my duties, never to let any of my buddies down, and not to do anything to a German I'd regret later.

MARSEILLES

Nine **days later in** the early morning hours of December 6, I sighted the Rock of Gibraltar from the port deck. The huge mountain of limestone rose up on the horizon like the horn of a unicorn. The backside of the promontory was dense with trees, but from my far away view, it looked covered in moss. Excited and anxious, my hands trembled. I took a deep breath and exhaled, thinking it was only a matter of a few days before we'd join the fight.

Two days later at sunset, we sailed into the harbor at Marseilles. Just three-and-a-half months earlier the Seventh Army had joined the French Resistance forces and liberated the famous port city. I gazed at the seventeenth-century buildings and cobblestone roads from the ship's deck as we anchored about a mile away, hoping I'd get a chance to tour the historical town.

The next morning after breakfast, I headed for the deck. Way up in the distance, the highest point in Marseilles was the gold dome and glowing green limestone of the famous Notre-Dame de la Garde (Our Lady of the Guard) Catholic basilica;

what a gorgeous site. The bright morning sun was illuminating the entire area surrounding the enormous structure.

Boraff and Gulley got my attention. I pointed toward the Basilica and enjoyed their amazement before following them to our platoon meeting below. It took a couple of hours to unload our gear, then we loaded into trucks and followed the 232nd Regiment through town and then along a dirt road for about two miles to Command Post 2, CP2, our new home in Marseilles, a skull-shaped hill that looked like Golgotha. I jumped out of the truck, and the fierce wind blew right through my jacket and uniform. We huddled together between the trucks, hoping the wind would cease. It never did and continued as we unpacked our gear.

Later that afternoon we broke numerous stakes trying to pitch our tents on the rock-hard ground. Setting up camp, I noticed things had changed. We were all aware of being vulnerable to attack. Everyone was on edge. The following night Sergeant Marcinek tried to lead a group to pee on a fire when the sound of a small aircraft surprised us. It seemed hilarious at the time. The next day Lt. McLaurin decided we needed some R&R. He divided us up and sent six men to spend a night in town each night.

Unfortunately, Mingus, Gulley, and Boraff were not in my group. I'd hoped to visit some of the great buildings in Marseilles with them, but I was with Sergeant Ervin's group, and they were only interested in finding French prostitutes.

I followed behind Sergeant Lewis as we marched toward the city, passing a large marketplace and bazaar filled with tents housing Arabs and their women. We stopped near a tavern where Ervin and Lewis got directions to a brothel. I slowed my pace up the long hill, falling behind the troop of five fast-marching soldiers on a mission. I was a reluctant straggler. I had no desire to have sex or make a romantic connection in this war-torn town.

Finally, there it was on the hilltop, a two-story house

with a red light. Ervin and the others double-timed it up the stairs to the porch then inside the front door. I followed and entered a large, smoke-filled, Paris-green-colored room with several oil-stained tan couches and antique corner tables and lamps. Many GIs were waiting, most with a drink in their hand, crowded around the cloth-covered chairs and sofas—it was standing room only.

My eyes stayed focused on the hardwood floor as French music played from an old radio. I stood next to Lewis, who seemed to enjoy the festivities. He elbowed me, downed a shot of brandy, and called me a bore. I just smiled and shrugged. Then a frail, middle-aged woman with rose-tinted face powder caked on her cheeks and wearing bright red lipstick approached us. I turned away before making eye contact, embarrassed by the entire spectacle.

"Who's next?" she asked.

Lewis jumped at the chance.

I muttered, "Good-bye," and slipped out the front door where a new group from the 242nd had gathered. Sergeant Ervin was on the steps outside talking to a young lady. I gestured with my hand and murmured that I was heading back to camp. Ervin looked at me and then ignored me. I hurried to the street, thinking this was not for me.

A few minutes later, it had turned pitch-dark, and I could barely make out the roof lines of the houses along the street. I stepped quickly down the hill, thinking about Mingus's warning to me about GIs being found with their throats slit. Then I thought about those wicked, long knives carried by Arabs at the bazaar just up ahead. I decided to walk in the middle of the road, listening for threatening sounds, moving cautiously in the still of the night. When I saw the silhouette of *Golgotha* on the horizon, I let out a sigh of relief and picked up my pace. I presented my pass to the MP at the entrance gate and headed for our tent.

everal days later and late in the afternoon, a troop
train arrived in Marseilles to take us to the front. The
following morning a thunderstorm blew in. I stood in
the mess tent after breakfast, dreading walking into the cold
rain and howling wind, thinking, *This is a bad sign.* Looking
around at my fellow soldiers scarfing down biscuits and scrambled
eggs, I noticed most of them had grown beards. We'd
changed over the last week in more ways than just grooming.
My buddies' faces looked more serious now. Maybe it was our
proximity to war or what lay ahead or because we'd heard stories
about dead American soldiers loaded onto the transport
ships that had delivered us to this war-torn country.

The self-evident truth was that some of us would be heading
home dead. I said a prayer then, that we would find the
courage to do the job here and that our families back home
would find peace. Then I thought about Albert. I couldn't
bear the idea of letting him down. I remembered Mom's letter
saying they prayed for my safe return every night. I wanted to
see my family again. I couldn't let myself think about never
seeing them again.

Pulling my jacket together and zipping it up, I headed
through the canvas flaps exiting the tent and met the calm
after the storm. I walked slowly, enjoying the absence of wind

on *Golgotha*, when thoughts about the front intruded. The journey had begun, and some of us were going to die; it was hard getting that reality out of my mind. I told myself I had to keep moving forward, thinking about the future, knowing I had a purpose.

I met Mingus and Gulley in our tent, and we talked while packing our gear. Gulley knew about the transport train. It consisted of forty-and-eights, boxcars so named because each could hold forty men or eight horses.

We lined up out front, backs to the wind, which had returned, and Lt. McLaurin addressed our platoon. He asked if anyone could use a hammer and saw. I raised my hand. He motioned me forward, led me to a pile of boards, and handed me a carpenter's saw.

"See if you can cut out a toilet seat."

I didn't understand. He explained he needed a seat with a hole that would sit on a five-gallon can.

Oh yeah, I thought. *Each box car would need their own latrine for the train ride.*

I went to work cutting a hole in a board with a carpenter's saw, which was not easy. Once I got the cut started, I discovered I could bend the saw blade slightly. I made four lids in short order then smoothed the rough edges. Lt. McLaurin was impressed.

With our rifles, ammunition, backpacks, and field camp supplies, our entire regiment marched into town, and our platoon of thirty-eight men loaded into a single boxcar. We stood shoulder-to-shoulder, front-to-back like sardines, standing room only.

I said to Gully, "Forty? Eight." He turned away, shaking his head.

Our train eased out of the station then accelerated to cruising speed, the train's steel wheels clicking like clockwork every ten seconds when they hit the rail joints. Noticing a large box of K-rations behind me, I scraped the wax off the top of the box and made a candle, using a string for a wick. Hours later after sunset, twilight turned to darkness through the crack in the door. I lit my candle, creating a glow in the middle of our boxcar, and enjoyed the moment until someone said: "Put that damn light out."

Sergeant Ervin announced it was time for sleep. "One, two, three—all down."

Everyone hit the floor except me, still standing with my candle. Men were packed all around my feet, leaving me no sight of the floor. I blew out the candle, stretched out across the bodies below me, and fell asleep.

Two-and-a-half days later, I'd stopped dreading arriving at the front. Anything would be better than this boxcar. Human beings really can get used to anything. I would have never thought it possible. I'd slept standing up along with many others in our platoon, leaning against one another. But it wasn't quality rest. I could see the effects of sleep deprivation in Mingus's droopy eyes, and he was the toughest guy I knew. We were all exhausted, and the two-fingered whistled sounds of excitement by several in our platoon reflected our collective relief as we pulled into the final train station south of Strasbourg.

I joined Gulley and Boraff near the ticket box in the station. We checked out the Christmas decorations: a spruce tree decorated with handmade ornaments near the conductor's office, a circle of garland on a table surrounded four lit candles, and a ceramic nativity set. Pine branches were twisted into two large wreaths on the wall.

It was Christmas Eve. After dinner, Gulley, Boraff, and I got permission from Lt. McLaurin to attend Mass. We got directions to a place of worship. Arriving a few minutes before midnight, we followed a troop of French women wearing veils into the Gothic-style church with large, arched stained-glass windows, a raised altar with a rectangular oak table, and behind the altar a gaping hole in the stone wall at least ten feet in diameter, partially covered by a purple drop cloth.

An elderly man approached us. "Hello," he said. "Follow me."

He led us to a pew down front, explaining the hole in the wall had been caused by an errant friendly artillery round.

"Sorry," Boraff said.

The man smiled and shook his head. "The allied forces liberated us, giving us new hope. Merci! Thank you!"

A French priest came out of the sacristy and joined us. Boraff knew enough French to ask about Communion. The priest agreed to let us celebrate provided we confessed our sins to the first English speaking priest available. We celebrated a beautiful Latin mass, Communion, and thanked the elderly man sitting beside us. We slipped out the side door, greeted by more snow.

We rejoined our platoon at the train station, invigorated that we were here to save these wonderful people. I had a lift in my step as I grabbed my gear from the boxcar and headed for the staging area where we would board trucks carrying us to the front. We huddled together during the early morning hours in the bitter cold, twenty degrees below freezing with eight inches of snow covering the ground and more large flakes falling, sticking to my eyelashes. I'd never been this cold before.

About an hour later, dawn broke; I'd never been so happy to see that large orange ball of fire and warmth in my life.

"It's Christmas morning!" someone yelled.

I thought about my family back home in Chattanooga and thanked God that they'd been spared from what the French people had endured.

A few minutes later, we loaded into open trucks with as many men that could fit standing shoulder to shoulder in the back. When we started moving, the wheels threw snow all over us, and the wind cut through my four layers of clothing like a knife through butter.

We hit a hole and our truck almost flipped. The entire group staggered trying to hold on. Piazza, the guy next to me, was almost ejected. He grabbed my neck and stepped on the foot of Gilberto, who flew into a rage and tried to reach for the trench knife in his boot. Thank goodness I was close enough to prevent him from reaching it. Piazza couldn't apologize fast enough, and after a few moments passed, calmer heads prevailed.

I believed Gilberto would have stabbed Piazza. We'd been pushed to the limit, living on *Golgotha,* sleep deprived, the long train ride, limited K-rations, brutal wind, and the freezing cold had used up all of our reserves. And we still had a long way to go.

About five hours later, we stopped for a bathroom break. It was so cold I hated to get out. Exhausted and frozen stiff, I walked behind the pine trees to pee. About eight from our platoon joined a troop of ten from another platoon who said they were going to start a fire. They headed for a wood-shingled house about a hundred yards away, up a small hill.

A short time later, I heard screams and stared in shock— the house was ablaze. Two women and four young children had rushed out of the house screaming and crying. A window exploded, and yellow flames billowed toward the roof. A lump formed in my throat. I wanted to run and help them, but I knew it was futile. The women desperately threw snow on the flames. I couldn't believe what I was witnessing.

Those poor people, now with no home and no clothes. Everything gone—and on Christmas Day.

The men returned and silently loaded onto the truck. I looked down at my boots not wanting to make eye contact with the guys who'd set the house ablaze. I jumped in after them, and we continued toward the front, bumping up and down in the back of the truck. I looked around at the oval faces of my fellow soldiers. Sergeant Ervin met my gaze and grinned. His smirk stepped all over my grief. He'd said nothing—done nothing—to stop it. And we could still hear the screams and crying in the distance.

Lt. McLaurin had joined the officers and ridden ahead of our convoy. I knew he would've stopped it. I watched the flames and plume of black smoke fade into the distance. What was happening to these great young men who I'd trained with at Gruber and who I knew were decent human beings? I pulled out my Novena and read *The Third Day*. I directed my attention to the goodness of God and prayed for mercy, for all.

We traveled by truck for another five hours. It was slow going in the snow, traveling on dirt roads, zigzagging through rugged terrain. At twilight we turned off the main dirt road and followed a small dirt track to a concrete wall. We jumped out of the trucks, and I immediately stretched my arms and legs, yawning. About a hundred feet ahead on the right was a large concrete fortress built into a hill. Sergeant Jodrey led us around it and called it a fortification and part of the Maginot Line. It was mostly underground with only a turret visible from the other side of the hill.

The French built the fortifications, weapon installations, and troop housing facilities to stop a sudden invasion, slowing the Germans and buying time for the French Army to counter. The Line included France's borders with Italy, Switzerland, Germany, and Luxembourg.

Boraff looked at Gulley and muttered that the Line didn't extend to the English Channel and had led to Dunkirk.

I didn't understand. "How?"

Boraff responded that the Krauts had attacked unexpectedly through the Ardennes, a thick evergreen forest with small mountains and white water rapids located in Belgium, exploiting the weakness of the Maginot Line. They'd blitzed into France and trapped the Brits against the sea at Dunkirk.

We marched through steel double doors, down some stairs, and into a hall. It was clean, warm, and well-lit with polished concrete floors and white-painted brick walls and ceiling. To my delight, we entered a large room filled with the aroma of warm food where a wonderful Christmas dinner was waiting for us on serving tables. Mess Sergeant Marcinek carved a ham. I grinned, happy to see his mug. It was the first meal of the day. I grabbed a tray and loaded my plate with turkey, dressing, and gravy and sat on the floor next to Sergeant Lewis and Private Piazza. Our body odor almost defeated the smell of the delicious grub, but I didn't care. I gobbled down my plate and went back for seconds.

McLaurin brought out a mail bag, and Gulley called out the deliveries. I got a Christmas card from Mom, Dad, and Albert with a letter from Mom talking about how much they missed me and were praying for me every night. She said that Albert led the prayers no matter what, and he couldn't wait till I'd be able to come home. I also got a card from several of my high school classmates. They were praying for me too.

I joined Mingus and Gulley for apple pie then the lights went out, and we lay with full bellies on a cold concrete floor with a roof over our heads, munching on pie. I closed my eyes, prayed for the homeless family, turning them over to the care of God, and fell asleep.

The next morning, I awoke early and wondered what was next. I read from my Novena, *The Fourth Day*, and felt grateful I was loved by my family and that they were safe in America.

The cooks served us hot cakes and eggs. I grabbed a cup of coffee with my breakfast and talked with Lt. McLaurin as he ate hot cakes. He was just a couple of years older than me. He loved talking about the Citadel. He was a great person who cared for each soldier under his command. He'd come from a family of soldiers. I shared that I had too. I was so glad he was leading us.

We loaded into our trucks that morning and drove to

Strasbourg. The city I'd been waiting to see had dirty snow pushed into mounds on cobblestone streets lined with multistory buildings, brown and beige French Tudor row houses with stucco gables. Many of the windows had candles. They'd decorated the tall gas streetlights on Main Street with garlands and red ribbons. We stopped on the road, got out, and stretched. I walked ahead toward a steeple.

The grand Notre Dame Cathedral had the highest steeple in town and stood as a singularity, a monument of beauty with its large, Gothic-style windows welcoming sunlight from all sides. At that moment the arched, stained-glass windows, pink sandstone, and copper roof reflected a shaft of sunlight that had broken through the clouds. Transfixed by nature's spotlight on human capability and triumph, I gazed in awe, knowing I could not have captured a more beautiful and meaningful view if I'd visited this town a thousand times. It was truly inspiring, human capability and our pursuit of God.

We set up camp just outside the city. For the next two weeks, we loaded into trucks and traveled to a different town along the German border, wanting to give the German Army the impression that more US troops were arriving every day.

It turned out that the Germans had led another offensive through the Ardennes and were threatening to cut off the Allied supplies at Antwerp. A thousand German tanks were hitting the 101st Airborne at Bastogne, Belgium, with everything they had, hoping to advance onward to Antwerp. Command called it the Battle of the Bulge.

Aweek later our entire company, about 120 soldiers, had moved into a castle next to a river that ran through the property. The mountain stone chateau had two towers and a turret facing the water. The dining room and ballroom had large chandeliers, stone fireplaces, and an adjacent balcony overlooking a couple acres of grassland and a dense evergreen forest.

I moved into a foxhole a few yards from the water along with Private Piazza, my ammo man. Below our position on the riverbank was a flock of ducks that occasionally erupted in quacking and squawking. Piazza and I talked for several hours, getting used to the episodic quacks. He was a married man in his thirties and terrified of being killed and leaving his family behind.

The ducks flapped and squawked, interrupting us. We moved in silence and grabbed our rifles, preparing for an attack and listening for enemy troop movement. About twenty minutes passed with no more flapping or any sight of German troops. We agreed to split up watch. One of us would sleep for two hours while the other watched. Piazza took the first watch.

The ducks would not leave him alone. They started quacking about ten minutes later, and Piazza woke me believing the Germans were attacking. I switched with Piazza and watched while he struggled to sleep. This went on all night; neither he nor I slept a wink.

At daybreak Piazza said that he wanted to check on a foxhole next to us. I watched as he wandered several yards into the woods and disappeared. I looked for him that morning. Later that afternoon during lunch, Boraff told me that Piazza had broken down in tears, and McLaurin sent him to the rear.

"He missed his family," I said. "He didn't want to die."

"Piazza broke," said Boraff.

"Yeah, he did," I replied somberly.

Piazza would have been a liability in combat, no doubt. I was glad he would get to go home. Then I thought about McLaurin. He understood the men under his command and looked after us.

A few days later, we entered the town of Ingolsheim, about forty miles north of Strasbourg. We relieved a group of soldiers who told us that we were lucky to be there; they hadn't seen a German in several days.

Gulley and I watched them load into trucks, and as they were leaving, Boraff approached and said, "They jinxed us."

At midnight the Germans hit us with tanks striking a small railroad depot about five-hundred yards from town, where we'd placed a squad to make sure the rail was secure. In the surprise attack the tanks blew the top off the depot, sending flames a hundred feet into the night sky.

Our platoon rallied, and Lt. McLaurin led as we jogged behind him schlepping through frozen snow to rescue the squad. We followed a frozen creek that ran alongside the rail and took up positions about one hundred yards from the burning building. I lay on gravel that supported the train track, warming from depot flames, and could hear the slow *clack-clack* of a German tank's track. It started over the creek bridge, hesitated, pulled back, and waited. McLaurin believed they were afraid to commit because they had no idea about our armaments.

We gave cover fire as the depot squad, exposed by light from the fire, ran toward us. The tanks' machine guns riddled the ground as eight zigzagging squad members made their escape. We stood our ground, and the two tanks quickly retreated. They had no idea that we were there without artillery support. We didn't even have a bazooka.

McLaurin gave us bad news as we marched back to Ingolsheim. Our company had lost our first soldier in battle; PFC Gillum had been killed at the depot. I remembered him from boot camp and our war games at Gruber. I imagined Gillum's smiling face as we walked with heavy steps. *Was he just a memory now? What was his meaning?* I also wondered about his family, knowing his mother would soon be getting the devastating news.

I returned to my squad's shelter for the night, an old vacated barn, and struggled to sleep on the straw-covered ground. Finally, I drifted off, then woke a couple of hours later, hoping it wasn't true. The reality of Gillum's death consumed my attention. I wanted to destroy the Nazis. The war had become personal.

By late afternoon we'd created a line of resistance—shallow foxholes near Maginot-Line pillboxes just outside of town. I joined my squad of eight in a pillbox and could see a column of German soldiers in their white winter uniforms moving toward us, about six-hundred yards away. Feeling outraged, I left the pillbox and opened fire. I wanted to kill them all for what they stood for and what they were doing to the world.

When I noticed concrete chipping off the pillbox just above my head, I realized that the Germans were returning fire and their bullets arrived faster than the sound from their muzzles. My heart pounding, I hurried for cover inside. They wanted me dead too, in an aggressive, arrogant, and impersonal way. It dawned on me—I was in a war—standing in the way of the German war machine.

We let them have it then from all sides with .30-caliber machine gun fire, blistering their infantry. They spread out and exchanged fire. We'd put them on their heels. When darkness came, we had to make a decision. Since we had no artillery, Command decided we should fall back into another Maginot Line fortress, which was about a mile-and-a-half on the other side of town. Our retreat would leave Ingolsheim to the Krauts.

Later that night McLaurin told me to pick two men and go scout the area between the town and fort. I looked at Boraff and Gulley who'd heard McLaurin ask me to scout, and they both stepped up. At about nine o'clock, as we readied to head out, a jeep carrying a Catholic chaplain arrived. I ran to meet the chaplain, walked with him, and confessed my sins. The chaplain told me that my penance would come in the form of whatever awaited me on patrol, but he assured me that my men and I would come back safely.

Gulley, Boraff, and I headed into the swirling snow. There was at least a foot on the ground and more blowing in our faces. As we moved out of town, everything got very dark. The rolling hills faded into the murky horizon. I turned around, and the lights of the town had dimmed. I believed artillery from another outfit south of us was firing on German positions to the north, and I could see enemy artillery in the north firing south of our position. I decided to use the artillery as my reference.

About thirty minutes later, we'd found the Maginot Line fortress and started back. But the combination of darkness and the blizzard conditions disoriented me. I was totally lost. I had no idea which artillery was ours and which was theirs. I asked Gulley and Boraff if they knew where we were, and they both shook their heads, looking dejected. I thought about the chaplain who'd told me my penance. I wondered if perhaps God had found my sins more serious than he did.

We continued trudging through the snow, freezing, totally lost, and thinking we'd be captured or killed any minute. Gulley heard some voices, and we dropped to our knees, grabbing our rifles from our backs, and crawled in the snow toward the sounds. I clutched my rifle, finger on the trigger, stopped, and waited until Boraff signaled all clear. He'd known by their voices they were American troops.

Gulley yelled that we were from the 222nd, lost, and needed help. They welcomed us with flashlight beams, scanning our uniforms, then lowered their rifles. We'd found a squad from the 242nd stationed a couple of hundred yards from where we started. We made it back and led our group to the fortress south of Ingolsheim.

The next day we heard that the 101st had held out at Bastogne, and Patton's Third Army relieved them; the thousand German tanks had not made it to Antwerp. We celebrated the great news.

We rarely got news. I'd never seen a copy of *Stars and Stripes*, and I'd never seen a reporter. Most of our news came from replacement troops and mail. We never knew from one day to the next what we'd be facing. We just knew we had to keep moving forward, pushing the German frontline all the way back to Berlin. Tonight, some in my platoon believed that Hitler would probably turn his attention to Northeastern France where we were.

We ate **K-rations, dug** foxholes, waited for the Germans to attack, and at night slept on the cold, wet floors of the fortress just south of Ingolsheim. On our third night, Lt. McLaurin called us all together and told us that Captain Bellum had ordered us on a combat patrol into Ingolsheim. I glanced at Boraff and then watched the blood disappear from Gulley's cheeks. We knew what it was like scouting at night in this terrain. McLaurin said he'd told Bellum it was a foolish idea, a suicidal idea. But Bellum's orders stood as issued.

Damn! I thought. *Bellum's going to get us all killed.*

McLaurin told us he would not hold it against any man who chose not to go on the patrol. Silence filled the large, poorly-lit concrete room. I grabbed my gear and ammo. Mingus grabbed my ammo magazines from me, saying that he would be my ammo man. The other men followed Gulley and Boraff, grabbing their weapons.

As we headed toward the door, a soldier appeared with a mailbag. McLaurin halted our group and asked Gulley to pass out the mail. I got a letter from Dad. He knew I would have to face some hard moments ahead and wanted me to know I had his eternal love. I almost cried reading his timely and heartfelt words.

McLaurin held up a letter and read a long list of soldiers' names from his Citadel class who'd lost their lives in the war. When he got to the end of the list, he paused and looked around at each one of us.

"McLaurin will be the next name on that list," he said. "Let's move out."

I brought up the rear and noticed Gilberto was the only soldier who'd decided to stay behind. We headed across the snow-covered fields toward Ingolsheim and spread out like we were in a long skirmish line. I led the right flank with Mingus, Gulley, and Boraff—the toughest and most fearless soldiers in our platoon. We had a little moonlight, which was good and bad, providing a horizon for direction but also making us targets on our enemy's horizon.

We came to a small creek about ten yards wide and searched for a place to cross. Sergeant Jodrey found a narrowing and waved at us to follow. I walked behind Gulley. We carefully stepped down the three-foot bank and onto the ice. It creaked and cracked, shifting beneath our feet. I jumped to the bank and climbed up to a field covered with a foot of snow, noticing about sixty yards in front of us was a tree line.

We were all bunched together where moonlight reflected off the snow. When I turned to find Sergeant Jodrey, all hell broke loose. A German machine gun nest in the tree line had opened fire. I hit the ground, my face buried in snow. I lifted my head a few inches and bullets were flying everywhere. I saw tracer bullets lighting up in every direction. The German gunner was whipping his rounds back and forth left-to-right and right-to-left.

Lt. McLaurin wriggled backward in the snow and said that we were in deep trouble, all bunched together. We heard soldiers' boot movement in the trees while the machine gunner reloaded. It was clear they would flank us and massacre us all in a matter of minutes. We were visible to that gunner and his rifle support, and for the moment paralyzed by their cover fire.

McLaurin told us that Jodrey was dead. Mingus crawled over and wanted to rush the damn machine gunner.

"No," McLaurin said, and shook his head. "No."

Lt. McLaurin ordered us to retreat when he threw his phosphorus grenade. That would be our signal.

The Nazi gunner was plowing up snow, whipping his .30-caliber rounds back and forth just in front of me. I couldn't move, or he'd pick me off. I wanted to give cover fire. Mingus managed to shoot a few rounds. McLaurin had moved quickly, wriggling through the snow, and within seconds, we heard an explosion lighting up the countryside with a pure white light, brighter than an acetylene torch. The Germans hit by McLaurin's phosphorus grenade screamed in pain, in agony—primal screams that I'd never heard before.

They'd ceased firing, and we retreated as ordered. We crawled, jumped down, crossed that creek, and ran as fast as we could. When we reached the next tree line about two hundred yards from the creek, we stopped to catch our breath and regroup. I looked toward the others, performing a head count. I asked Gulley if he'd seen McLaurin. He shook his head.

"Did anyone see McLaurin?" I repeated. No one responded. "We've got to go back for him."

Boraff came forward. "McLaurin's dead, Dorris. That Nazi machine gunner got him when he raised up to throw the grenade."

My mouth gaped, and my eyes filled with tears.

"McLaurin's dead. He made his last throw—a throw we'll never forget," Sergeant Ervin said. "Let's move out."

I wanted to break down and cry, cry my heart out. McLaurin had saved our lives from certain death. We'd made a mistake crossing that creek, and McLaurin had given his life for us. In grief with heads low, our platoon of twenty-seven struggled back to the fortress, knowing our beloved leader and friend was no longer with us. And we'd lost Jodrey, who I'd never forget.

We returned to the fortress reeling from our losses. I tried to sleep, but couldn't. I read my Novena, *The Ninth Day*, and prayed for my platoon and for all of our families. I thought about McLaurin for a long time and the long list of Citadel officers who'd died in this war. I closed my eyes, and the memory of the machine gunner firing at us played in my mind.

Alive one day and dead the next. No one cares, I thought and quickly realized I was being cynical. I couldn't let myself go there. I had to stay positive. McLaurin had given his life for our freedom. He'd fulfilled his purpose. He would want all of us to carry on our journey, giving our 100 percent effort to defeat the German Army.

A few minutes later, I wondered what end I might come to. What would be the meaning of my life? Finally, I fell asleep.

Our entire platoon looked bedraggled and disoriented as the new day dawned. That morning and all day, we built foxholes preparing for an attack. We had to carry on. We had to keep moving forward. And so we did for the next four days, with Sergeant Gee directing our digging.

Having finished my new hole, I stood up and gazed toward Gee, who was about fifty feet away, when a German tank round hit directly in front of him. He was killed instantly, his body decimated. In shock, I dove for cover as machine gun fire filled the air. The tank gunner hit and killed Private Smith as he ran toward my hole.

Sergeant Camp located the tank, which had been painted white to blend with the snow. We launched grenades and tried to hit it with mortar fire, but it slipped away.

It rained all night, melting the snow. The next morning we located the tank that had killed Gee and Smith and called in an artillery strike, blowing that white panzer to smithereens. It felt good to see that tank destroyed, but it didn't diminish the loss of Gee and Smith.

Later that day a flame-throwing tank approached the fort to our right inhabited by a platoon from the 242nd. We couldn't call in an artillery strike because the tank was too close to them. We couldn't help those soldiers; they had no chance. I wondered if they were the soldiers who'd helped Gulley, Boraff, and me when we'd gotten lost.

We watched in horror until the platoon finally surrendered. The tank's flames would have incinerated many of them and asphyxiated the rest by burning up all the oxygen. We pulled back and joined a line of resistance, and oddly the Germans retreated.

That night, we got news that the frontlines were changing, and we were needed in another sector. We loaded up in trucks and headed to Neubourg.

OPERATION
NORDWIND CONTINUES

"*Dorris! Dorris!*" **Mingus's words** broke through my unawareness. I woke from my daydream to the external reality, peering over the front sight of my rifle into swirling fog. The taunts of German infantry and the creaking rollers of panzers approached. Our flares had lit up the battleground, and they'd advanced to within two-hundred yards.

Sergeant Ervin ran past us, yelling, "Fire! Fire!"

Mingus fired, turned a few degrees, and let off eight rounds in that first minute. I could barely make out a target in the fog. The Germans looked like ghosts darting back and forth. I pulled the trigger and shot off twenty rounds in less than twenty seconds. Mingus was all in, firing all over the horizon. I continued firing bursts in automatic mode. A few minutes later, I stared mesmerized by the hellacious fire power of the machine gunners on the left side of our line. They had tracer bullets flying all over the battlefield.

A giant explosion grabbed my attention. We'd fired mortars striking a panzer and jeep with a mounted machine gun about one hundred yards away on my left, their exploding munitions lighting up the combat zone like a Fourth of July fireworks display.

We heard the turret of a tank turning.

"Get down!" yelled Mingus.

I ducked to the icy floor of our hole, both hands clutching my helmet, holding on for dear life. The tank blew off the top of a tree on our left then blew a hole in a section of forest to our right. Our mortars hit back wounding the tank, and it retreated.

We got up slowly and continued firing. I went through two magazines in about two minutes. My rifle barrel was smoking hot. I had to calm down and get in the fight. The plan had been for our platoon to lure the Germans, to draw them in, so they'd try to flank us in the clearing, the firebreak on our right. We had a heavy machine gun platoon with two M2 Browning .50 calibers waiting in the trees on the other side of that break.

"Dorris, hear that?"

"What?"

"Paratroopers are leading those panzers, and they're using burp guns."

Burp guns were like hand machine guns that could fire about five hundred rounds a minute, making a burping sound when they fired.

"Yeah, I can hear them."

"I'm going to get one of those guns."

Aiming, I fired in semiautomatic mode at swarming paratroopers who were trying to get a drop on us from our right flank. My rifle barrel was still smoking hot. The fog was lifting, and moonlight reflected off the snow. Suddenly, Mingus and I were in the firefight of our lives. All hell was breaking lose. Those damn Krauts were almost on top of us.

And the guys on our left were about to be overrun. I directed my fire in their support and saw Sergeant Ervin grab a paratrooper and kill him with his knife. I turned toward the tracer rounds and smoke on my right and simultaneously heard our .50 calibers firing. They unleashed hell on what looked like an entire company of German infantry supporting a couple of panzers headed toward the clearing.

The sounds of death and devastation erupting from those two M2 .50 calibers shook me to my core. I watched in awe. They punished those Nazis for about twenty minutes until they'd had enough and retreated to the forest. We'd paralyzed one tank, and a soldier charged it, climbed up, flipped open the turret hatch, then let 'em have it with his machine gun. I gazed at Mingus, who was reloading his M1 rifle.

"Ma deuce!" he said, meeting my eyes and shaking his head in amazement. "That's firepower."

"Those M2s are unbelievable."

"They're beasts in combat," he said, and glanced toward a couple of dead Germans about twenty yards from our foxhole. "Ma deuce!"

I'd heard M2s on a firing range at Gruber, always firing away from me, but I'd never heard any weapon sound and fire rounds as terrifying as those machine guns had on this battlefield. Their devastating, lethal firing bursts had arrived just in the nick of time, like a cavalry riding in and saving us from certain death. I thanked God for that platoon.

I was so thirsty. I grabbed my canteen and took a long drink of water. Mingus took a swig and ate some chocolate and handed me half a bar. Oblivious to the freezing temperature, we munched and relaxed for about thirty minutes until the Germans returned to attack. I looked over at the blanket and realized there were only two magazines. I still had six on my belt, but I needed to conserve ammo. I fired in semiautomatic mode while Mingus fired about five rounds a minute. I nudged him and warned that we were going to run out of ammo. Then our heavy machine gun platoon opened fire again.

We watched as our .50 calibers unloaded on German paratroopers, punishing them. Mingus shot at a couple of Krauts in snowsuits, snipers on the ground trying to take out our machine gunners. I turned my weapon toward them and let out a burst of fire, silencing them. The Germans had lost a lot of soldiers trying to take out those M2s. Finally, they retreated.

About an hour later, we heard a tank coming up the road below the firebreak. We watched a squad from the heavy machine gun platoon take one of the .50 calibers to the road. Somehow the Nazis had gotten in behind us. Mingus guarded our rear, and I kept my eyes up front. The Krauts attacked again, and we punished them again. The .50 caliber on the road stopped the attack from the rear.

We held them again and then again.

At about 5:00 a.m. Mingus and I were down to about forty rounds of ammo between us. Sergeant Ervin told us to hold out one more hour then we were going to fall back on the road behind the firebreak where trucks would be waiting.

Time slowed down that last hour. Exhausted and cold, we heard the moans of wounded all over the battlefield and watched smoldering fires of burning vehicles and debris. I fired half a magazine at a sniper who'd hit a couple of our guys retreating through the clearing.

Dawn broke over the trees on the other side of the firebreak. Ervin and our squad pulled back first. Mingus and I stayed and gave them and the others cover. About twenty minutes later, Mingus and I headed through the woods stepping over fallen trees and through craters created by the German artillery. We made it through the snow and bushes to a road and looked around.

We saw not a single soldier or truck. Thinking we'd made a wrong turn, we ducked back into the woods. Suddenly, one of our transport trucks appeared. We jumped out and waved them down. Relieved and overjoyed, I followed Mingus, and we climbed aboard the back of the truck. A sergeant from another platoon told us that we'd held the Nazis off long enough, and elements of an armored division had arrived to take over.

Grateful that we'd prevailed, I took a seat next to Mingus, removed my helmet, sighed, and then directed my attention to thanking God. A few minutes later, I pulled out my Novena and read *The Ninth Day*. My mind drifted to McLaurin and the meaning of his life and all the others who'd made the ultimate sacrifice.

We **drove to a** small French town of several thousand people, parked, and unloaded from the trucks. On one side of the street naked chimneys overlooked rock piles and charred lumber, and on the other side rock and stone row houses with beige stucco gables stood intact.

Sergeant Ervin assigned our squad to live with an elderly French couple who'd taken in war orphans. We entered through a slate foyer with muddy boots and gear and advanced into the kitchen where we met the weary faces of an elderly couple and four small, skinny children with large eyes, clinging to the couple's legs. The man told us to settle anywhere we liked. He, his wife, and the orphans would live in the kitchen and basement.

"Merci, merci," we replied.

I led Cedrick, Bloss, Mingus, Gulley, Boraff, Wade, Ostrowski, and Gilberto up the stairs where we found a balcony area suitable for sleeping and two bedrooms and a bathroom. I took a sofa in the balcony area and stretched out. Mingus waved and called for me to come with him to scout the town and grab some food. Our unit's kitchen crew would not arrive for a couple of days.

Always hungry, I got up and followed, bounding down the steps. Walking through town we saw dirty little children and frail old men and women. Merchants sold rations and water out of the back of trucks. I asked Mingus how long we'd be here. He thought we would probably stay a week, waiting on replacement troops and ammunition.

Walking past a farmer's market area, we watched some troops help themselves to some red meat, potatoes, and a case of wine. The shop owner yelled and cursed at them as they walked away.

The soldiers had fought in a hellacious firefight for these people and believed they were entitled to anything this town had to offer. I understood what was happening. All of their pent-up emotions from last night were coming out now as entitlement. I felt the same way. The town owed us. They had no idea what we'd just gone through. But I also realized that wrong was still wrong and never justified.

Mingus headed into a bakery and came out after a few minutes smiling with a couple of loaves of bread under his arm. A young girl with dark hair and large dark eyes, wearing a dirty, torn dress, stood on the street corner holding a plucked dead duck by the neck asking for dollars. That duck was bigger than she was.

Mingus and I were hungry, and I thought that duck might taste pretty good with gravy. Approaching with a grin, I offered the little girl seven dollars for her duck. She smiled from ear-to-ear, revealing her missing front teeth. She handed me the duck, grabbed the money, and skipped down the street. I'd given her my last dollars, and I didn't care. She was so happy. Besides we'd get paid in a few days. Once a month I got twenty-five dollars in cash. The others got fifty dollars. I'd signed for the paymaster to send half of my money back home for my future.

After three hours of boiling that duck in an old can in the French couple's fireplace, Mingus, Gulley, and I munched on the tender, delicious meat and sopped up the greasy gravy with bread. Shortly after eating, we fell asleep on the balcony.

All three of us awoke about the same time, vomiting violently. I'd never felt so nauseated; seasickness was nothing compared to this.

The kitchen came up the next day, but we were too sick to eat. The following day we felt better and made up for lost time with some of Sergeant Marcinek's turkey, gravy, and apple pie. We brought the orphans extra rations, crackers, and candy. The old couple seemed very appreciative, and the children grabbed our legs hugging us. So we brought more crackers and rations and convinced others to give to the orphans. We presented them with a large stash of goodies on two more occasions.

Meanwhile, we'd gotten some new replacement troops, and Sergeant Ervin paid us a visit and said that we'd have to pick a replacement for McLaurin. I hated to think about it. Col. Fellenz had told Ervin that the platoon needed to vote for either Kallaher or me to become McLaurin's replacement. The guys wanted me to be promoted, but I told them I preferred being the right wingman in our skirmish line. Nevertheless, we voted, and I lost by one vote. So Kallaher got the lieutenant field promotion. I appreciated the support from my buddies, but I didn't believe I was the man for that job.

Before sleep I read *The Seventh Day* in the Novena and prayed for Kallaher, our platoon, and all the war orphans.

The next day we loaded up in trucks heading for the Haardt Mountains of Germany. I sat in the back of the truck and noticed the old French couple we'd stayed with were going from truck to truck. When they found me, they asked me to follow them. I jumped down and walked behind them to their home, wondering what was up.

They led me into the living room, and the old man pulled the china cabinet away from the wall and pulled out a big bottle of schnapps. His wife approached with three glasses. The old man poured all three glasses to the brim. They gave me a toast. And I drank the first schnapps I'd ever had, burning my throat all the way to my stomach; then a warm tingle spread over my body. With tears running down their cheeks, the French couple hugged and kissed me. By the end I was crying too. I thanked them for helping us and the orphans.

On the way back to the truck, I realized how much our small generosity had meant to them. I guessed we'd given them hope. *Hope for what?* I asked myself. Then it dawned on me. *Hope that love might return to this war-torn world.*

I hopped in the back of the truck and with an inner smile, enjoyed reflecting on our toast and final good-bye once more.

Riding in the back of the truck for a couple of hours, we entered southwestern Germany. Boraff explained that we were closing in on the *Wehrmacht*—the unified armed forces of Nazi Germany. Like a prize fighter in a championship boxing match, we needed to proceed with caution. Because we had the Wehrmacht on the ropes, they were more dangerous now than ever before. With their backs to the wall, they would fight to the death. Boraff added that they probably had experimental weapons in the pipeline; we would soon become their guinea pigs. Mingus agreed.

I knew they were right, but I hated to think about what lay ahead. I pulled out my Novena and read *The Eighth Day.*

Our trucks stopped on a hilltop, and we got out to stretch. I walked over to the edge and could see miles and miles of the dense Haardt forest of pines, spruce, and a few beech trees. There were bald spots, sandstone, and rugged terrain. A V-shaped valley lay just below. I didn't want to think about German soldiers or what we would soon face. For the moment, I enjoyed the beauty of nature, hoping I'd be around to see spring.

Driving another thirty minutes, we arrived at base camp and relieved another outfit that had fought for every mile of this advance into Germany. They were happy to see us.

Ostrowski and I picked a nice foxhole already dug into the side of a hill with a roof over it and a view of a farmhouse and barn in the middle of a barren field. After a few minutes in that hole, I noticed a dead Kraut soldier lying about seventy-five feet from us. His face looked like spam. Ostrowski suggested he'd probably been part of an assault on this position. I agreed and turned my attention to the house and barn, wondering what had happened to the family who lived there.

We ate K-rations for dinner and spent most of the night talking. Ostrowski had a wife and two children, and he loved them very much. He had earned a black belt in judo. I told him about my family and my friends at school. Around midnight I got sleepy. I slept first, and we rotated watch through the night—two hours of sleep and two hours of watch. Ostrowski never bothered me. I slept on edge but pretty good.

The next morning we decided to take turns going over the hill to the kitchen for breakfast. Ostrowski went first. Those damn Krauts sniped and fired mortar rounds at him. I let out a burst of fire, half a magazine, in the direction of a German sniper. I looked over my shoulder, and Ostrowski had made it over the hill.

Damn, I thought. The Nazis seemed to know he was going for food, and they'd tried to pick him off. They were watching us and wanted to break our spirit. Ostrowski came back, and it was my turn. I wriggled out the back of the foxhole, rolled to my feet, and zigzagged as mortar rounds exploded in front and behind me. Then sniper fire ricocheted off the ground beside me. I made it over the hill in a few seconds as if I were a kid running as fast as I could from Billy and Tommy Daniels.

When I reached the mess tent, I saw a dead soldier's body covered on a stretcher. I hated to look. I pulled back the blanket and saw the pale face of Private Bloss. A sniper had killed the kid. Reeling, I proceeded into the mess tent.

Having lost my appetite, I grabbed some juice and coffee and sat at a table by myself. I read *The Ninth Day* in the Novena and prayed for Bloss and his family.

I finished my coffee, gathered courage, and headed over the hill. I zigzagged all the way back, but they didn't fire at me. I crawled into the foxhole, thinking the damn Krauts were probably trying to get into my head, so I wouldn't zigzag the next time.

I found Ostrowski's eyes and told him about Bloss. Neither of us knew too much about the kid. I remembered he'd donated his crackers and candy to the orphans. I prayed again for his family and hoped they would find peace.

For the next week, we stayed in our foxholes and dodged mortar and rifle fire every day and every meal. On Friday Ostrowski came running back from dinner and told me that Captain Bellum had decided we needed to patrol at night.

Damn, I thought. *Bellum.*

The next night our squad went on patrol. We started in a single file then spread out, forming a skirmish line. We walked and climbed over the rugged terrain, staying clear of the house and barn, which we knew were booby-trapped. We found signs of a German patrol or perhaps a trap. I had a bad feeling about this patrol.

Sergeant Ervin didn't want to follow their trail and ordered us back to camp. On the way we climbed up a steep bank and decided to take a break. Cedric was about five feet away from me when he sat down and triggered a shoe mine. The damn mine fizzled but didn't explode.

Cedric's eyes bulged out of his head, as big as saucers, and he murmured, "Shit."

Even though it was a cold winter night, I broke out in a sweat.

The mine fizzled more and then stopped.

"Don't move," said Sergeant Lewis.

Lewis made sure the fizzing had stopped then cleared

everyone away from Cedric. Then he stretched out his rifle; Cedric grabbed the butt of the gun, and he yanked him up.

No explosion.

We all let out a collective sigh of relief. We marched single file back to camp and slept all day.

The next night on patrol all I could think about was stepping on a damn shoe mine. We patrolled every night for a week and then spent a week back in the foxholes. I hated night patrol.

All had gone well for the last two weeks in our foxholes, and spring came early. Ostrowski and I had become good friends, and last week the Nazi snipers had retreated, making the trek to our meals an enjoyable experience.

Wednesday, we knew something was up when our entire platoon was ordered to the mess tent for an early afternoon feast. The kitchen had prepared a huge meal, turkey with all the trimmings and apple pie for dessert.

Boraff, Mingus, Gulley, and I filled our plates and chowed down at the same table.

"Beware, the ides of March," Boraff murmured, chewing on dressing and gravy.

Tomorrow is Thursday, March 15, the ides, the day Caesar had been murdered. I figured Boraff was probably right that a big battle was coming. We were due for action. Then right on cue Captain Bellum and Lt. Kallaher stood in front of our platoon. Bellum announced that we'd be launching a major offensive on the German lines. It was going to be a big push with all elements of the Regiment involved. Kallaher said that he'd brief our platoon tonight.

Gulley met my gaze and shook his head.

"You were right, Boraff," Mingus said, and kept eating.

"I knew, shitfire! Shit! I knew it," Boraff replied in disgust.

I understood the reality of an offensive in this terrain. We would lose a lot of men. At that moment I stopped chewing and prayed for my friends. Then I ate until I was stuffed, trying to suppress the thoughts about what we'd be facing. I got up and retreated to a private spot by a beech tree where I stretched out on the ground, lying on my back in the cool, soft grass, looking up at the billowing white clouds and beautiful blue sky. Feeling the warmth of the sun embracing me, I drifted toward sleep when a little songbird began to sing from a naked branch above. Relaxing and listening to the first bird of spring, thoughts of the war and our coming big battle left me. I felt a connection to the bluebird and realized I'd almost made it to official spring—

A shot rang out and I reacted, rolling over for cover, and searched for the shooter.

Gilberto stood on the other side of the tree with a smoking gun. The songbird was dead, his feathers blowing in the wind.

Gilberto laughed. "I guess I shut him up."

Saddened, I rolled back over and looked toward the clouds, wondering what we had become.

That night we met with Lt. Kallaher. He went over the battlefield plan, and the Germans had the high ground. We were assigned to assault an area of rugged terrain. We'd have to climb a steep hill to launch an attack on German machine gun and sniper positions. It sounded bad.

It was late when the briefing ended. Gulley, Boraff, and Mingus went to sleep. I couldn't sleep, so I stayed and talked to Sergeant Chipolski and Private Wade. Chipolski thought Bellum had picked another suicide mission for us. Wade turned to me and said this would be his last battle. I didn't say anything. I hoped he was wrong.

I made my way back to that beech tree, sat in the grass,

and read my Novena by flashlight. I read *The Eighth Day*, trying not to think about what the ninth day might bring. I prayed for my family, all my fellow soldiers and their families, then headed to my tent and fell asleep.

At daybreak, we marched in two lines toward a steep hill, and following behind our troops were a half-dozen unenthusiastic donkeys loaded with ammunition, braying up the rear.

Our attack started with an artillery assault, then we spread out and hurried up that hill, pulling ourselves up by grabbing small tree trunks and stumps. Once I'd made it to the top, I looked down from the precipice and smiled. Those stubborn donkeys had stopped and wouldn't budge; the ammo had fallen off the back of one.

I turned toward the next target—a tree line and dense forest area about a thousand yards ahead. I took the lead position on the right wing of our staggered skirmish line. There was a replacement soldier behind on my right. Gilberto was directly behind me, and Cedric was behind on my left. I walked cautiously on a dirt road as we approached a cluster of trees ahead. My rifle was loaded and my index finger on the trigger.

A rifle shot rang out, echoing off the sandstone mound on the right; the replacement soldier had been hit and was down. I dropped to the ground and clung to the earth unsure what direction the shot had originated from. Three more shots rang out. Then I knew the sniper was in the cluster of trees.

He'd hit my helmet with the third shot, knocking it against my face. The concussion blast felt like I'd been smacked with a wet dishtowel.

I thought this was it, my end. I felt my face and head, and I wasn't bleeding. I tried to lift my head, and he shot close. The bullet ricocheted a few inches from my head. I prayed and said an Act of Contrition and a Memorare—a prayer to the Virgin Mary—with my face in the dirt. The sniper knew I wasn't dead. I asked the Blessed Mother to go ahead and get it over with. I was ready to die.

"Please, quickly," I said under my breath.

Two minutes later, four 105 mm rounds exploded one after the other about two hundred yards from me, near the cluster of trees, shaking the earth. I looked up. Those artillery rounds had obliterated the sniper, ending the threat. I stood up and saw Gilberto's body behind me. He'd been shot in the face beneath his nose and killed instantly. I thought about that little songbird.

Poor Gilberto.

I looked over at another soldier and another, both dead. That sniper had killed three soldiers with four shots. Private Stangle approached and helped me back to the rear. I must have appeared in shock or dazed. He took me up to the Battalion Command Post on top of the sandstone mound. I sat on a rock, and Stangle kept asking if I was okay. I nodded and drank some water from his canteen.

When I gazed around the Command Post, I saw Col. Fellenz and beside him a helmeted commander, who was surveying the battlefield through binoculars calling in artillery strikes. When the helmet turned, I saw two stars and a silver scarf around his neck. It was General Harry J. Collins. Hollywood Harry had called in the artillery strike that saved my life. Rejuvenated, I convinced Stangle that I was fine, and we got back into the fight.

I zigzagged as German machine gun fire erupted,

running as fast as I could toward some cover brush, and passed the dead bodies of Sergeant Chipoloski and Private Wade where they'd fallen trying to reach cover. I lay in the brush and remembered Wade telling me that this would be his last battle. Wade had fought in the Aleutian Islands before joining the Rainbow Division. It was as if he'd given up hope the night before. Their deaths appeared to be related; they'd lost a vision for their futures.

I fired on the machine gunner as more soldiers from my platoon surrounded him, taking out the rifle squad supporting him. Mingus rushed the right flank and got the machine gunner. We'd taken out the machine gun nest and taken over the tree line.

Sergeant Ervin came by and ordered us to break and eat. I sat down on the ground by a log and opened my box of cheese and crackers. Glancing around as I chewed, I noticed a dead German soldier about four feet from me. I'd been totally oblivious to his presence. In combat your mind was trained on motion and movement; anything perfectly still was usually not an active threat. I noticed the dead soldier's face didn't have whiskers. Shaking my head, I turned away, thinking about his family; he was just a kid.

Suddenly, a tank opened up on us. I rolled next to a tree and heard the whistling sound of a 75 mm cannon round heading straight for me. *I'm dead*, I thought, then everything happened in slow motion. The round hit the tree and shrapnel hit me in the right leg. My entire derriere went numb. I was afraid to reach back and examine the damage, thinking part of me was gone.

Our artillery took care of that tank, and a medic arrived and tore my pants open. He looked at the wound, cringed, and quickly wrapped a bandage around my thigh and hip. He asked if I could walk. I thought so. The feeling had returned in my leg along with a burning sensation about a hundred times worse than any road rash from a bicycle accident. I got up, and the medic helped me limp toward the aid station.

When we got to the steep hill, the donkeys were still refusing to climb; the GIs tasked with encouraging them were drenched in sweat. Perhaps those donkeys were smarter than we thought. I leaned on the medic as he practically carried me down the hill.

The doctor in the aid station took one look at my wound and ordered me into an ambulance along with five other wounded men. We drove for hours to reach a hospital somewhere in France.

I woke the next evening to find a man in the bed next to me crying. A psychiatrist came in and talked to him, explaining he would have to return to the front. The poor guy cried harder, and I wished I was a thousand miles away. The young soldier had cracked under artillery fire. I could relate; I'd almost cracked myself, enduring a solid hour of German artillery, mortar, and rockets.

Five days later after twice-a-day dressing changes and lying prone the entire time, I was allowed to get out of bed and walk. The hospital was a large complex connected to a convent. I figured there was a chapel somewhere on the grounds and got directions from my nurse. I thanked her and found the heavy, brown door at the end of the hall. I walked into the large, dark, empty chapel, the only light coming from a small window high on the left wall, illuminated by afternoon sunlight. The light fell on a small statue of the infant Jesus. The only other light was from a flickering vigil candle close to the altar.

I knelt to pray, and a sense of tranquility and warmth embraced me like the welcoming open arms of God. I was in the presence of my maker. I knelt in peace and love for a long time, not wanting to leave. But the hip pain returned, so I stood for as long as I could then headed back to bed. I visited the chapel every day for the next four days, experiencing the calm and love of God.

On the tenth day, my doctor discharged me and said I was fit for battle. I boarded a truck with other repaired soldiers and headed back to the front.

On the way we stopped to let a soldier off. His unit was sitting near the dirt road, eating rations—then one of the men blew up. The pin in the hand grenade in his pocket must have fallen out, causing it to explode and blasting his hip to smithereens. I stared in disbelieving horror. Blood squirted from the gaping wound; a medic ran over and put a pad over his injured side and hip. There was nothing anyone could do. The soldier collapsed and died.

We loaded back into the truck, and all my serenity, all my spiritual cash, had been stolen.

What purpose? What meaning? I asked myself in frustration. I pulled out the Novena and read *The Second Day*, then I prayed for all of our families back home.

W hen I got back to my company, I found them camped in a small pine forest bordered on three sides by a winding river. Boraff and Gulley met me with smiles and warm embraces and filled me in. The guys had some great stories. Mingus had made the Browning automatic rifle man in another squad. Then he'd attacked a German machine gun nest trying to get a burp gun. He failed, and his right arm was wounded in the process. They'd heard he would never fire a gun again and would be going home.

I knew that wasn't true and told them Mingus would be back. Gulley joked that Mingus wouldn't stop until he had Hitler's scalp.

I'd returned during Holy Week, so on Good Friday, Gulley, Boraff, and I headed into town, looking for a Catholic church. We spotted a steeple and made our way through an alley and across the main street. We entered the quiet church and placed our rifles and helmets against the back wall. We walked quietly and seated ourselves in a pew. About twelve women seated in front rows turned toward us. They looked angry. One little lady stood, appearing agitated. She pointed toward us and spoke loudly. Another woman stood and pointed at us too.

The German priest came down from the altar and appeared to be chastising the women, who listened and appeared ashamed. I hated to be the center of controversy. I knew it must have been hard for these women seeing American soldiers in their church as the war continued just outside. I knelt and prayed a few minutes for these women and their families and then the three of us headed out, grabbed our helmets and rifles, and went back to the world at war.

On Easter morning we loaded into trucks and drove toward the front, passing dead Kraut soldiers' bodies on the side of the road. Sporadic rifle fire erupted several times as we approached a small German town. We unloaded, and our entire company advanced in two lines into town, then down the main stone street. Kallaher had instructed us to search houses for hiding German soldiers and to take out any pockets of resistance. He'd also advised us that snipers were all over the place, so we needed to advance cautiously.

Searching for and collecting prisoners all day and late into the night, I was beat. We'd killed one sniper who wounded one of our men. We'd taken about thirty prisoners. My squad took over a nice house at the end of town, and I slept on a bed for the first time since I'd been wounded.

The next day we became pros at rooting out pockets of resistance and could quickly search a home pulling enemy soldiers out of basements, attics, closets, and from under beds. We had a system for taking captured Germans to a collection area in the rear where they would be processed.

Losing a couple of our company to a sniper in the next town, some of our soldiers became enraged at the German soldiers we caught. A couple of guys in my platoon took prisoners into the woods, and their prisoners were never seen again. When I asked one platoon member what had happened, he replied that the damn Nazis had tried to escape. I didn't believe him and looked away, shaking my head.

In the next town we were supposed to hurry before the Germans could destroy a bridge. I was only fifty yards from the bridge when the earth shook, and our entire platoon hit the dirt just in time. The explosion scattered pieces of the bridge at least a hundred feet into the air, the wooden remains raining down all over us.

We went around that town and approached another community. I followed a beaten path to the top of a hill where I could see down into a valley ahead of us. I saw a passenger plane fly off after an aborted landing. I looked for a runway, but apparently the pilot had tried to land in the field to rescue someone. As the plane flew away, a German soldier jumped on a bicycle and started peddling down a dirt road. He was almost beyond my rifle range, about six hundred yards. I fired a burst in front of him, and he slammed on the brakes. He turned and headed back in the opposite direction. I fired in front of him again, and he wheeled around. When I fired again, he stopped, threw his rifle down, and dropped his bike. He put his arms over his head and walked toward me.

I climbed down the hill, keeping my rifle aimed at him, and took the soldier prisoner. To my surprise, he was an officer. Thinking he might have some valuable information, I marched the German captain into town where Captain Bellum and Sergeant Camp conversed near a truck. I noticed some new replacement troops nearby. I approached Bellum and told him about my potentially significant prisoner, but he didn't listen to me. Instead, he turned toward the replacement troops and motioned for a new arrival named Private Wanvig to come over.

Bellum looked Wanvig in the eyes, and said, "Private, shoot this prisoner."

My jaw dropped. I couldn't believe my ears.

"Private, I gave you an order, and you are on my battlefield."

"No, sir," Private Wanvig responded.

"Private, I gave you a direct order. Shoot him."

"No, sir," repeated Wanvig. "Sir, permission to speak, sir."

"What is it, private?"

"I cannot carry out an illegal order, sir."

I almost cried. Wanvig had brought me back from the darkness of war. I didn't know if I would have had the fortitude to say no to Bellum if he'd ordered me to shoot the prisoner. But I did know I wouldn't be able to live with myself having carried out such an illegal order against humanity. At that moment, I wanted to hug Wanvig.

Finally, in frustration Bellum ordered another replacement soldier to take the prisoner to the rear. I walked away, my mouth still gaping. I met Gulley and Boraff and shared K-rations with them, explaining what had happened.

"Bellum is crazy, Dorris," Boraff said.

Gulley found my eyes. "He's a madman with power. Stay away from him, Dorris. I heard a couple of guys talking about wanting to take him out by accident."

I sighed. "He relishes his power over us and the prisoners." I was so grateful he hadn't asked me to shoot that German officer.

After dinner Gulley passed out the mail, which had come with the new replacements. Mom had sent me a box of cookies for Easter with several letters, referencing all those who were praying for me after I was wounded. Albert had taken the news very hard. Dad had convinced him that I was going to be okay. I almost cried thinking how hard it was for Albert to understand what war was all about. His innocent clarity hindered him from understanding the insanity of war.

That night we found a warm place to sleep, a barn full

of black and white dairy cattle, Holsteins. I wrote a letter to Albert telling him I was okay, then curled up in the straw using my box of cookies for a pillow and drifted to sleep. An hour later I woke with a rat's tail tickling my cheek as it pursued Mom's cookies. I gave up the cookies, thanked God for Wanvig, then drifted back asleep.

As infantry, we didn't pay much attention to the skies as long as our Air Force controlled them. Our company marched in two lines heading for Wurzburg. Gulley was in front and Boraff across the road. Sherman tanks and halftrack vehicles loaded with infantry troops passed us by as the sun set on the horizon. In the distance the sound of airplane propellers approached, and soon British bombers had filled the twilight sky, heading deeper into German territory. Their formations spanned from horizon to horizon, as far as the eye could see, their steady roar too loud for us to talk over.

We'd been blessed with air supremacy since before the Battle of the Bulge. Now we faced a new battle for Wurzburg, a city of about 100,000 people. As darkness fell we found a barn, settled for K-ration suppers, canned meat, bullion, a biscuit, sugar, coffee, a cigarette, chewing gum, and thanks to Gulley, a little red wine. He'd picked up a bottle in the last town and explained that we were in a special part of Bavaria, wine country, and we'd earned the wine. Boraff and I sipped from the bottle as we lay stretched out on straw. It didn't have the punch of schnapps, but it delivered a warm tingle.

Lt. Kallaher came over to brief us on our role in the coming assault at Wurzburg. I asked about the bombers we'd seen, and he said that they were probably heading for Berlin. They'd already bombed the hell out of Wurzburg. Kallaher said that they'd hit it hard with explosives and incendiary devices. Reports indicated the city had burned rapidly. We should expect to see rubble and smoldering ashes. Our first job would be to secure the area around the old Wurzburg Castle and then find a way across the Main River as soon as possible.

A wave of sadness washed over me. I looked over at Boraff, who'd told me about the great churches of Wurzburg built in various architectural styles: baroque, Gothic, and Romanesque. I hated to hear that those famous, grand, ornate churches hundreds of years old with their arches, high ceilings, and large chapels had probably been decimated or burned to the ground.

The next day we took a small town and rounded up about a dozen prisoners. Gulley, Boraff, and I went into a house to check for more German soldiers when I heard the whistling sounds of bombs falling. They were heading right for us. That panic I'd felt in the foxhole with Mingus near Neubourg returned. There was no place to go, no place to hide. I looked out the back porch window as the ground and house shook, throwing me to the floor.

I jumped up and peeked out the shattered back window and saw three bombs sticking half-way into the ground. My heart skipped a couple of beats until a few seconds passed, and I knew the bombs weren't going to explode. I called out to check on Gulley and Boraff. They ran into the kitchen, and their jaws dropped when they saw the bombs.

We hurried out of that house to the street and headed for our rallying point. All three of us would have been killed if those bombs had detonated. I slowed my pace, thanked God, and began reflecting on all my close calls; there were too many to count. I thought, *How will this end for me?* and wondered how many more lives I had. Before I could imagine my ending, I realized I had something important to do. I was here for a reason. *We were here for a reason*, I told myself.

With that thought playing in my mind, I walked faster to catch up with my buddies. Our kitchen crew had caught up with us, and the three of us got in line, savoring the smell of warm turkey and dressing.

The next day at twilight, we rode tanks during our final approach to Wurzburg, a city Gulley said was famous for fine wines. A violent storm raged in the distance, with lightning flashes and rumbling thunder. The tanks dropped us off at the edge of a cliff looking down on the Main River. High on the hill to my left, was the old Wurzburg Castle, a sprawling, fortress-like, medieval structure with turrets on every corner surrounded by a large rock wall. The Main's bridges had been destroyed, and our soldiers were crossing the river in pontoons pulled by ropes attached to pulleys. Looking more closely I realized they were using German prisoners to pull the pontoons. And those prisoners were being shot at by their own troops, with shells exploding in the air and all around the boats.

The Germans deserve that duty, I thought.

I gazed toward a hill on the other side of the city and saw the flashes of a great gun, probably a mile away. I hurried over to a tank crew and led them to the cliff's edge. They saw the big gun and proceeded to fire three 75 mm cannon rounds toward it. I watched as the rounds exploded short of their target. Suddenly, the tank revved its engine and rushed back in reverse.

When it dawned on me what was happening, I chased

after the tank and hit the ground. Within seconds that huge German gun had fired several rounds exploding near us. One round hit a tree, and a large limb fell on top of me. I lay there thinking: *How many more lives do I have? I need to be more cautious.*

I got to my feet, dusted off, tested my legs, and then saw my platoon was heading for the river. We loaded onto a pontoon. That big German gun had stopped firing, and I smiled. I guessed we'd scared them away. Reaching the opposite bank, we stepped ashore quickly and met a welcoming line of GIs. They were passing out bottles of champagne, wine, and boxes of vanilla wafers to every one of us. The soldiers said that they'd robbed a warehouse down the road. I looked at Gulley, who was smiling.

The GIs directed us toward the next block where the shooting was still going on. I put my box of cookies and champagne on the side of the road and ran toward the rifle fire. A squad from another platoon had already silenced a sniper when Boraff and I arrived. We spread out and started a sweep across the city. It really had been destroyed, just like Kallaher had said. Blocks and blocks of nothing but naked chimneys, the rubble of walls, fractured bricks, and debris strewn all over the streets.

We ran from chimney to chimney, from rubble pile to remnant walls attacking German soldiers who fired at us. I ran fast and covered a couple of blocks where a sniper was firing. I ran into a building and up a flight of stairs hoping to reach another building to take out the sniper. It was a dead end. I found a window and dropped about ten feet to the ground below then found myself surrounded by a ten-foot fence made higher by steel bars on top. I was trapped like a bird in a cage, and rifle fire was coming at me from the front and side.

Panicked, I realized the only way out was over the fence. With the weight of my rifle and ammo, I didn't think I could do it. But I believed I'd be dead in another minute if I didn't try. I said a quick prayer, then jumped with all my might and reached my arms as high as I could. I grabbed a bar and pulled myself over the fence as bullets flew over my head; one ricocheted off the top bar. I collapsed on the ground and wriggled for cover behind some rubble as bullets ricocheted off nearby bricks. I lay as still as possible, catching my breath, and thanked God for giving me wings. When Boraff and Gulley came to my rescue and got that sniper, they looked like angels that God had sent to save me.

We fought on in the city famous for wines and captured a lot of German soldiers. It seemed surreal that one minute we were fighting, wanting to kill each other, and a few minutes later, they'd surrender, laying down their weapons. I'd captured about a dozen German soldiers and was escorting them back to the POW drop spot. I was walking beside my prisoners when another soldier approached, catching my eye. I took another look at him.

"Carter Broyles!"

He stopped and looked at me. "Jim Dorris—what in the hell are you doing?"

"I'm taking prisoners to the drop-off," I said, halting my troop.

Carter was a former classmate of mine at the University of Chattanooga, and we'd trained together at Gruber. We talked about old times in Tennessee and promised to make time in the future for a reunion with some of our mutual friends back home. Before we parted, Carter told me he'd tell our friends that he'd seen me if he got home first, and for me to do the same.

"Take care of yourself. I look forward to our future reunion back home." I smiled and waved good-bye.

Late that night I dropped off some more prisoners and

headed down a lit street to my platoon's rendezvous. We needed to decide where we were going to sleep. I noticed Sergeant Camp all alone under a streetlight, sitting at a table beside the remnants of a cafe. He took a swig from a bottle of champagne and placed it on a table near two empty wine bottles and a box of vanilla wafers. He appeared drunk.

I called out to Camp. When I got within about twenty feet, he opened fire on me with his Tommy gun. He shot left to right sending a burst of fire right at me. Bullets struck the street in front of me and the rubble behind me. I twisted in reflex trying to make myself as small a target as possible. Somehow he'd missed me.

"Sergeant Camp! Camp! It's Dorris! It's Dorris! Don't shoot!"

Heart pounding and my hands shuddering, I tried to remain perfectly still. Camp put down his weapon and picked up his bottle of champagne. I approached cautiously. He seemed to have no idea what he'd done. He'd almost killed me. And I had no idea how he hadn't from such close range.

"Sergeant Camp, what are you doing?"

"Dorris—shit! I thought you were a Nazi."

"You could have killed me!" I said, my heart still pounding.

"Sorry, Dorris." He swigged from his bottle then threw it, shattering it on the street.

Our rendezvous was a couple of blocks from here near the bombed-out bridge. I helped him up. He stumbled and headed in the wrong direction. All I could think about was whose idea was it to hand out champagne in the middle of a battle. I called out to Camp and redirected him. Thinking about how close he'd come to killing me, I waited and walked behind him. My hands were still shaking.

I must have something important to fulfill, I thought. *How did Camp miss me at point-blank range?*

The next night, we'd made it through Wurzburg, reaching the outskirts of the eastern part of the city. Lt. Kallaher chose a farmhouse for us to bunk in, and unfortunately, it was my turn to pull guard duty. The elevated road about ten feet above the level of the house appeared to be a good place to keep watch. Gulley and Boraff helped me dig a foxhole beside the road about 90 feet from the house. I thanked them when we finished, and they headed for the farmhouse.

I opened my box of K-rations and nibbled, preparing for a long boring night. It was a long four hours getting to midnight, and I'd fought off sleep several times. *I'm almost done,* I thought. *One more hour until I get relief.* I rested my head on a blanket and a few minutes later heard the distinctive sounds of German hobnail boots and voices approaching.

My heart pounding, I grabbed my rifle and eased myself into a defensive position, flat on the ground. The night was so dark I couldn't see them. I knew if I started shooting, I'd not be able to get them all. They'd learn my location, and I'd be killed. My platoon slept quietly too many feet away and would be of no immediate help. But if the German soldiers turned toward the farmhouse, I'd have no choice but to open fire.

I held my breath and remained perfectly still, listening

intently. The Germans were within five feet of me. They slowed and then marched on. I exhaled a long sigh of relief, and twenty minutes later after my hands had stopped shaking, I said a prayer in gratitude.

I didn't have any trouble staying awake after that.

We moved on that next morning and took a small town, meeting little resistance. I ran across the back yard of a little white stucco house, and an elderly German woman, probably a housewife, came out onto her back porch holding a plate with a piece of chocolate cake. She held it up, making sure I saw it.

I made a detour. She handed me the plate with a fork. I munched on that delicious chocolate cake, savoring every bite of the creamy icing. I thanked the nice lady, licked my lips, and quickly returned to attack mode, heading toward rifle fire a few blocks away.

After all the snipers were silenced, we checked houses. I'd made my way through about ten and had found no German soldiers. Then I went into a stone and cedar shingle house and found a stairway leading to a basement that was pitch black. I turned away then heard a noise. I returned, pointing my rifle down the stairs. Finger on the trigger, I hollered for them to come out. Nothing. I hollered twice more.

I was about to fire a burst of .30 caliber rounds into the basement when a little blond boy and red-haired girl appeared at the bottom of the stairs. Their mother jumped in front of them, and another older girl peeked at me from behind her mother. They had a big German Shepherd guarding them that barked loudly when he saw me. I waved and headed out the back door. It made me sick thinking how close I'd come to shooting that mother and her children. I would have never found peace if I'd killed them.

I continued on toward our gathering area and noticed a statue near a church. It was a three-foot-tall Pieta, the Blessed Mother holding the fallen Christ. I'd passed many shrines to the Virgin Mary in open fields when we marched, many times finding recently placed flowers at the base of the shrines. I'd never had the time to stop while marching, but now I took a moment to kneel near the Pieta, putting my rifle and helmet on the ground, and prayed in gratitude that I'd not killed that woman and her children.

Boraff heard our next target would be Schweinfurt, then Furth, Nuremberg, and finally Munich. Gulley had heard the same from Kallaher. Munich, the city where the Nazis came to power, was the big prize, the pot of gold at the end of our rainbow. The city had a lot of people, about a million at one time. I figured there would be lots of snipers and resistors.

Early that morning of April 10, we marched toward Schweinfurt. I had a new ammo man, a skinny eighteen-year-old kid from South Carolina named Private Freeman. He'd cried after his first firefight in Wurzburg. I'd taken him under my wing and told him to stay close behind. After marching for about two hours, we decided to stop and eat breakfast.

We split up and searched a small group of houses, hoping to find some eggs and bread to supplement our rations. Sergeant Lewis called us back to the road. Freeman had found some bread, but Gulley, Boraff, and I came up empty. We fell into two lines when Sergeants Ervin and Camp dragged a man from a house, and behind them a little, dark-haired girl followed screaming, "Papa! Papa!"

Ervin lifted the guy to his feet and held him as Camp approached, placed the end of his machine gun barrel on the man's forehead, and squeezed off a few rounds. The man collapsed backwards immediately, striking his head on the road. His skull came off, exposing his brain, steam rising into the frigid air from the sulci of his brain. I couldn't believe my eyes.

The little girl screamed in horror, waving her arms, yelling, "Papa! Papa!"

Ervin ordered us to march. Kallaher turned and moved ahead. My heart ached. There was no one to console that little girl. We marched onward, our appetites destroyed by the gruesome execution. It seemed like it took half an hour before we got beyond the screams of that little girl. I caught up with Sergeant Camp and asked why he'd shot that man.

He looked into my eyes. "He had an SS tattoo on his arm."

I looked down at the dirt road and saw the image of that little girl seeing her father executed. I prayed for her, mercy for her.

We approached a small town and met rifle fire from two different directions, about two hundred yards apart. We spread out and methodically surrounded them, taking out several snipers, and took ten German prisoners. I'd captured a big German lieutenant who must have been six feet five. He was dressed immaculately, his uniform perfect, and he even had a close shave. I felt embarrassed taking him prisoner in my dirty uniform. I turned him over to Private Lombardi, an Italian fellow from New York.

Freeman and I joined Gulley and Boraff for some K-rations and bread. We found a nice house with sheets on the beds. I ate canned meat and wrote a letter to my dad. Then I got on my knees and prayed for that little girl who'd lost her papa. I lay on my bunk, thinking of Dad, and fell asleep between the soft sheets.

The next morning we lined up and marched in two lines toward Schweinfurt. Lombardi marched across from me, and I asked him about the big German lieutenant. He looked away. When I asked again, he said that the lieutenant was a bastard. He pulled up his shirt sleeve and revealed about twelve wrist watches. He pointed to a steel watch with a black leather band.

"What happened?" I asked, and hoped Lombardi hadn't killed the lieutenant.

"I asked the German if he knew what I was going to do with him."

"Dammit, Lombardi! You didn't?"

"The arrogant German said I was going to shoot him. So I did. I shot him in the chest. But he didn't fall. He stared into my eyes. I shot him again, and he continued to stare. I shot a third time, and he fell."

"Shit!"

"But Dorris, all last night and this morning, I haven't been able to get that German's blue eyes out of my mind. When I close my eyes, I see his eyes."

"Good. Don't do it again! I mean it."

What had we become? I thought to myself. *We were becoming like the enemy. How do you destroy an enemy that hates you without becoming like them?*

We marched in silence.

About an hour later, a German machine gun nest opened fire on us, striking the ground in front and beside me. I hit the ground.

Bellum, who was about thirty yards behind in the woods, yelled, "Dorris, we can't hold the war up for you! Get up!"

Getting cover fire from Gulley and Boraff, I rolled and wriggled to a tree.

"Bellum, get your big fat ass up in front of these men and lead them instead of shouting at them," Col. Fellenz yelled to Bellum.

He'd appeared like an angel at the moment that Bellum had ordered me to stand up and take machine gun fire. I sighed and thanked God. Then I grinned at Boraff and Gulley as Bellum took the point. We outflanked the machine gun nest and moved to the next line. Bellum didn't want to advance anymore after that. So we rested till dark then found a barn to sleep in.

That night Lt. Simpson replaced Bellum. Boraff heard that Fellenz had demoted Bellum and sent him home. We spread the great news, and our entire company celebrated our liberation from Bellum. The guys were so happy. I felt like screaming at the top of my lungs. We were free. It was like we'd won the war. Boraff, Freeman, and I enjoyed several swigs of wine that Gulley had stashed in his canteen. Bellum was gone. I fell asleep as if the weight of the world had been removed from my shoulders.

The next morning we moved out. Two hours later while attacking a German line of resistance about fifteen miles before Schweinfurt, I ran through a plowed field, stepped into a hole, and twisted my right foot. I fell to the ground and lay there; I'd felt it pop and was afraid it was broken. Gulley helped me up, and throbbing pain ensued. I could bear weight on it, but I had to limp when I pushed off.

About twenty minutes later, I didn't think I could go on. We stopped to rest; I feared if I took my boot off I'd never get it back on. I marched onward and gave up my pain to the Lord as my mother had taught me. The pain eased, and my limp improved. When we reached the town, another outfit had secured most of it. We met little resistance, and since it was getting dark, Freeman and I looked for a house to sleep in.

We approached the side door of a stone and stucco house. We entered and found a large hall and a big kitchen on the right. On the far side of the room, there was a stairway leading to a balcony. I hobbled up the stairs and into a large bedroom. On the left side of the room, brackets extended out about a foot on both sides of the wall supporting a clothesline with all sorts of clothing. On the right was a large double bed. A lamp was lit on the table.

I was too tired and hurting too much to worry about the lamp. A large window overlooked the forest where the Germans had retreated. My ankle throbbed, and all I wanted to do was to get off it. I sent Freeman to get some food. I pulled an easy chair close to the large window, sat back, and elevated my foot on the windowsill. Immediately, the throbbing pain eased. I let out a sigh in relief.

The sound of a rifle's metallic click interrupted my moment. I turned around, and to my amazement, I was looking into the barrel of a gun held by an old woman who looked about seventy. Her cheek was against the stock of the rifle as she aimed at my head. She had a wicked smirk on her face. All I could think was: *She's going to kill me.* After all I'd been through, this would be my meaning.

She must have been hiding behind those clothes, and there was nothing I could do. She was out of reach. I stared at her face and made eye contact. After a long moment, the rifle began to waver back and forth, and she started crying. I got up slowly and took the rifle from her hands. She stood there with tears running down her face. I held the rifle in my left hand and used my right hand to reach out and pull her into a hug. I had nothing but deep sorrow for what she'd been through.

She buried her face into my chest, sobbing uncontrollably. Her head was four inches below my chin. I patted her back to calm her. She told me that German soldiers had given her the rifle and told her that Americans would do terrible things to her. I assured her we just wanted a place to sleep and some food. We meant no harm.

When I released her, she stepped back with a questioning look. I told her to go downstairs, and we would not bother her. I didn't see her again. The next day when we lined up out front in the street, I could see her peeking at us through a window. As we marched off, I put my hand up and waved good-bye in her direction. She gave a little wave, making me smile. I had a flash thought about how horrible it would have been for her and me if she'd killed me.

On **April 18 we marched** toward Furth and Nuremberg. Kallaher took the lead as we approached a block of destroyed buildings and what was left of a train station. The Allies' bombings had destroyed most of Furth's rails and leveled the inner city. We hurried through the city meeting minimal resistance and crossed into nearby Nuremberg where we met heavy resistance and decided to wait for our tanks.

About an hour later, we followed behind our tanks and pushed the Nazis back. Then we started the dangerous task of taking out the snipers one by one. We approached the bombed-out airport and ran in a skirmish line toward a couple of snipers hiding behind destroyed planes, attempting to surround them. I don't know how I ran on my right foot, but I believe the adrenaline rush from being shot at had a lot to do with it. When all was said and done, we'd captured about two hundred German soldiers and secured the airport.

Later that night we enjoyed warm food: turkey, mashed potatoes, and biscuits prepared by Sergeant Marcinek and our kitchen crew. We found some warm, soft spots in a bombed-out hangar. I propped my right foot up on a box of K-rations, and with a smile on my face, fell asleep.

The next day we went back and searched the rubble that

used to be Nuremberg for resistors and snipers. That night I had guard duty and stood outside a house where my platoon slept. At about 1:00 a.m. I heard hobnail boots coming toward me. I slipped behind the corner of the house, and when the German soldier passed, I shoved my rifle barrel against his abdomen.

"Halt!"

I scared the hell out of him. He broke into a sweat and begged me not to shoot. "I have a wife and children."

Throwing his arms in the air, he cried and put his head on my shoulder. I didn't know what to do. I thought about that time I'd captured Col. Fellenz during war games at Gruber. He'd warned me never to let a prisoner get close to me.

"Step back," I said.

The soldier was slobbering all over himself, snot coming out his nose. I took him to the POW drop-off area where he begged me not to leave him. I promised him he'd be okay. I looked Private Lombardi in the eyes, giving him a stern look. I reassured the prisoner he'd be fine and handed him over to Lombardi, who nodded and said that he'd take good care of him.

DACHAU

On April 18, we'd taken Furth then moved on to Nuremberg and captured the airport. We spent the next nine days cleaning up pockets of resistance around Furth and Nuremberg.

On the morning of April 29, we loaded up on tanks and rode south toward Munich, leaving our kitchen and camp behind. We stopped for a break, and the platoon commanders huddled around Col. Fellenz. A few minutes later, Lt. Kallaher approached, and we gathered round him. He said that we'd been ordered to liberate a former POW camp turned into a concentration camp at Dachau. In a way the guys were glad. With a million people living in Munich, we dreaded having to take out a lot of Nazi resisters and snipers there. Boraff thought it would be the hardest city we'd faced. I hated to think about it. Dachau seemed like a reprieve.

We hopped back on the tanks and rumbled down a long hill on a wide road named SS Strasse. We'd traveled about halfway down the hill when it became hard to breathe. A noxious, almost suffocating odor filled the air, a combination of rotting eggs, rotting cabbage, garlic, and human feces. I gasped and pulled my undershirt over my mouth and nose, taking shallow breaths.

We got off the tanks and started down a road parallel to forty-and-eights, boxcars. I looked inside the first one, and there must have been two hundred bodies stacked in the car, nothing but skin and bones, all dead. I remembered how crowded the boxcars had been for our platoon, when we rode from Marseilles to Strasbourg. I cringed thinking about the inhumane treatment that had led to their deaths. I walked closer, but the odor was too strong; I couldn't breathe. I trudged to the next car and found more of the same.

What in the hell had happened here? I asked myself and kept walking.

I moved on, passing boxcar after boxcar, the stench unbearable. There were forty cars. It was clear that someone had opened fire, killing the survivors on this train ride to hell. Bullet riddled bodies had fallen out of the cars, and other bodies trying to escape lay strewn on the road. I looked at the mutilated, decaying, rawboned bodies and had to turn away. I couldn't take it.

"Shit, holy mother of God." Lt. Kallaher's face twisted in anguish as he turned away too.

Gulley and Boraff's faces had turned pale, like a white sheet. My entire squad appeared in shock by what we'd stumbled upon. Just ahead, German Shepherds chained to the front gate were barking, growling in a frenzy trying to get at us.

I heard a couple of soldiers yell as they drove ahead in a Jeep with a .30 caliber machine gun mounted on the back. Boraff glanced at me and said that there had to be two thousand dead bodies. I couldn't hear myself think with those dogs going crazy. Sergeant Camp marched toward the gate and shot the dogs, and everything grew eerily quiet. A couple of guards in towers shot at the Jeep; our guys returned fire and killed them in a few seconds, leaving the guards' bodies stretched out on the ground in front of the towers.

Then an entire company of SS guards—all well-fed—came walking out of a side gate, their arms raised in surrender. The soldier in the Jeep lost it and fired his .30 caliber machine gun, mowing those SS guards down.

From out of nowhere, General Linden drove up and jumped from his jeep, yelling, "No! No! Cease fire! Cease fire!"

The soldier in the Jeep ran out of ammo and was crying. He'd cracked; it had happened so fast. We got the hell out of there when a couple of MPs joined General Linden and Col. Fellenz.

Lt. Kallaher and Sergeant Ervin proceeded through the main gate, and I followed close behind. There was an outer concrete wall around the entire facility. I estimated it was five acres or about six football fields. On the other side of the camp, there were barracks and old factories on property twice as large as the prison camp.

About fifteen feet inside the concrete wall, a high fence surrounded the entire camp.

Kallaher flipped a switch and shot through a cable carrying electricity to the fence and then made sure he'd cut the power by throwing the dead guard's helmet at it. Ervin ordered me to walk between the wall and the fence and not to let anyone escape from the camp. I walked cautiously and had gone about fifty yards when I came upon the dead body of a man who'd been horribly beaten. His left eye was laying out below its socket on his cheek.

On the other side of the fence, there was a long row of dead, naked bodies, probably a hundred or more. It appeared they'd been killed the night before. Looking up, I saw about two hundred starved prisoners, rawboned skeletons, standing on the gray dirt of the prison yard, staring at me. They stood perfectly still, not making a sound. A tall one broke away and ran toward a mound of dirt. Three other prisoners tackled him and tried to open his clenched fists. I thought they were going to kill him as someone had killed the man lying near my feet.

Raising my rifle, I wanted to shoot a burst of rounds over their heads. But I saw the barracks behind them and didn't want to hurt any innocent people. I glanced around at the emaciated prisoners and dead bodies everywhere. I thought: *I must be in hell.* In my imagination I could see the devil coming up from the ground. None of the war before had affected me like this.

In despair I looked at the sky and pleaded, "God, get me out of this place."

When I looked back down another prisoner with a swollen hand approached the fence and asked me if I had a cigarette. I had a couple of packs in my jacket pockets, but I was afraid if I brought them out I'd have a riot on my hands. I looked him in the eyes, shaking my head.

"Nein."

"Wait a minute," he said, and ran behind the barracks.

I looked toward the tall prisoner; they'd opened his fists and found nothing. The three had left him crying on the ground. The prisoner with the swollen hand reappeared and approached the fence. He pushed his hands through the links and gave me an old can. Inside I found a stained, old cigarette butt, perhaps an inch long.

"I want you to have this," he said, his eyes glistening. "My thanks for rescuing us."

Wondering what this human being ravaged by malnutrition and disease, having been exposed to horrific treatment and destruction in this death camp, could be feeling, I looked into his dark eyes twinkling with human love. Emotion welled up. He'd given me the greatest treasure he had. I shook his good hand, thanking him over and over. His gaunt face and sunken eyes lit up in joy; he'd been starved for human love. I'd made a new friend, and his capacity to love under these circumstances overwhelmed me. At that moment my entire attitude toward the prisoners changed completely. I knew God had answered my prayer. I waved to all the other prisoners, and they began to smile and wave back at me. I felt as though I'd found my meaning, my purpose. I was doing something great.

I put the can with the cigarette butt in my jacket pocket, knowing I'd cherish it for the rest of my life. The prisoners were told to return to their barracks. Ervin told me a hospital company was on their way. Private Stangle came and relieved me. I found his eyes.

"How could they have done this?" I asked, unable to really imagine what had happened here.

Stangle shook his head. "I never hated the Germans before this. Now I want to kill them all."

"I know," I said reluctantly. I didn't have another answer.

We watched as the hospital team arrived, served them a warm meal, and gave desperately needed medical attention. The prisoners were sick with typhus and infested with scabies and lice. I fought off an overwhelming rage toward the Nazis and prayed for the prisoners again.

I joined my squad and noticed a change. The guys didn't say anything. Many in our company couldn't wait to kill the Nazis tomorrow. They hated them for what they'd done to these human beings. Our kitchen came up that night and prepared a meal for us. Most didn't eat. The stench and horror of what we'd uncovered had taken away our appetites.

My squad was assigned one of the barracks for sleep. I joined Gulley, Boraff, and Freeman in the guards' bunk room. I walked over to lie on a lower bunk bed and noticed the cover thrown back and the pillow still indented as if the guard had just gotten up to leave. I lay on the bunk wondering what had happened to lead the man who'd slept here to do the things he'd done. I prayed for the prisoners, survivors, and those who'd perished that they and their families would find love and peace. Then I thanked God for delivering me from hell. Knowing we'd be fighting those responsible for these atrocities tomorrow in Munich, I fell asleep.

Waking early, I read *The First Day* of St. Therese's Novena, lying on the lower bed in the guards' bunk room. I got up and watched the sun rise over Dachau. A new day was dawning. I found the kitchen, grabbed some scrambled eggs, toast, and coffee then joined my squad. A couple of hours later, we loaded onto tanks.

I gazed one last time at the prison camp and stared at the boxcars, inhaling the scent of death. My eyes filled with tears. *I cannot go back there,* I told myself and forced my attention to focus on what lay ahead. Would I be alive for sunset? Would I see a new dawn?

Thirty minutes later, approaching Munich, I prepared to jump from the tank and lead the right wing of our skirmish line. No rifle fire. No resistance. We kept moving forward, not meeting any resistance. I looked over at Gulley and Boraff in amazement as tall, broken buildings of the sprawling city appeared on the horizon. To our surprise we rode into town and were greeted by cheering crowds lining both sides of the street. They threw flowers at us and handed out bottles of champagne to a few of the troops riding on tanks. I couldn't believe it.

I smiled and shouted to Boraff, who was sniffing a yellow rose, "We did it!"

"This is crazy," he said.

In the center of town, we jumped down from the tanks. Kallaher ordered us to begin a patrol of the city, which had been destroyed. Buildings over two-hundred-years old had been devastated, leaving nothing but shells of what they'd once been. The streets were almost empty. Most of the citizens had deserted their bombed-out city.

"Spread out," Kallaher said. "We've got a lot of ground to cover."

I headed down a wide, empty street and saw nothing nor heard any rifle shots for three blocks. I checked out a vacant single-story building—nothing. I returned to the street and heard a woman screaming in terror from a two-story office building just ahead on my right. I couldn't imagine what was going on. It sounded like something for the local police. But the screams got louder and louder, and I couldn't ignore them.

I ran into the building onto a beige tile floor and noticed mahogany office doors on both sides of a long hallway. I found a stairway on the far side of the building and climbed two steps at a time. The screams were much louder and coming from an open door just ahead. Holding my rifle ready to fire, I ran through the door into what appeared to be a waiting room. A lady who appeared to be about seventy stood just inside the next doorway, her hands covering her face, screaming in terror.

I rushed past her and into the next room where I saw a large, glass case filled with dental instruments to my right. Shocked by what I saw, I stood motionless and watched as one of my platoon buddies, Private Pettit, smashed the glass case with his rifle, spraying shards all over the place. In the middle of the room, an empty dentist chair faced a large glass window. In the far left corner of the room, Sergeants Ervin and Camp were beating an old fellow, a dentist cowering on the floor. They struck him with the butts of their guns. Ervin whacked the old man's head with a forceful blow, and then Camp kicked the poor guy in the abdomen.

I couldn't believe my eyes. How could they do this after what we'd witnessed at Dachau? Mingus had always said that Ervin was a cold-blooded killer. I figured he'd finish the dentist off with one more blow. Ervin not only outranked me, but he was also a brute, and he was far too good a fighter for me to physically stop. I'd seen him kill a tough German paratrooper with his trench knife on that hellacious night near Neubourg. He was a killer.

Ervin raised the butt of his rifle, getting ready to wallop the poor fellow.

"Stop it! I'll shoot!" I yelled. "Damn you, Ervin! I'll shoot the next one who hits that old man!"

Silence filled the room. Ervin and Camp froze and looked up at me in surprise. All eyes focused on me as I held my rifle pointed at Ervin with my finger on the trigger.

Ervin looked away, and said in a low voice, "Let's go, men."

All three walked right past me, looking straight ahead, ignoring my presence. My hands shook and my legs trembled. Even my body wasn't sure if I was bluffing. I believed in that moment of rage I could have killed him. I thanked God for delivering me.

The old dentist got up and moved behind me to hug his wife. I kept my eyes on Ervin as he and the other two walked through the waiting room, across the hall, and down the stairs. I turned to look at the old couple who were hugging each other tightly. The lady gave me a look of appreciation, which a thousand words could not have captured. I met her gaze and embraced her warm smile, letting my eyes speak my apology. She understood and her face relaxed.

The dentist, who I assumed was her husband, cried as he thanked me. After a long moment, I turned and walked out cautiously, hoping Ervin had moved on. I went outside and the street was clear. I scouted two more blocks and reached the banks of the Isar River, where Kallaher and the rest of the platoon had gathered.

Kallaher asked for five volunteers to go with him across a bridge into another sector. I volunteered as did Pettit and three others. We walked in a skirmish line for a couple of blocks, then Kallaher asked Pettit and me to guard a bridge. We stood in silence for about an hour before a tank came to relieve us.

Headed back to our rallying point, Pettit and I walked through a beautiful park that was like a botanical garden with tree-lined paths and blooming tulips: reds, pinks, white, and yellow. I looked at Pettit and asked what the hell they were doing to that old dentist. He apologized and said that Ervin thought the dentist would have a stash of gold used to fill teeth.

"He wanted gold?"

"Yes."

I shook my head in disgust, wondering how anyone could be thinking about gold after what we'd been through. When Pettit and I rejoined our platoon, Ervin and Camp said nothing. Gulley had found a place to get a warm meal, so Freeman and I joined him and Boraff, and off we went to a café on the other side of town.

Walking behind my buddies, I said a prayer in gratitude. We'd taken Munich without a shot, and I'd stood up to Ervin. I reflected on the moment I'd confronted him and Camp. I realized then a new freedom as I thought about Ervin. I was no longer afraid of him, which felt great, almost as good as when Bellum had been sent home. I revisited the warm feeling of love from the dentist and his wife and caught up with my buddies. I was ready to chow down on some Bavarian meat and potatoes.

W**e moved on, taking** several small towns, meeting little resistance. On Sunday, May 6, we were in Austria about thirty miles from the Brenner Pass, which led through the Alps into Italy.

It was late in the afternoon. We'd moved into a nice house, and I sat with Freeman, Gulley, and Boraff at the kitchen table contemplating dinner. Gulley wanted to eat *hasenpfeffer,* or rabbit meat, mashed potatoes, and gravy at a local diner. Freeman was sitting next to me, examining a German .38 caliber revolver he'd found in Furth. Gulley and Boraff sat across from us, discussing the different techniques they'd used to trap rabbits back home.

I heard Freeman pull the trigger, then an explosion, and knew that damn German .38 caliber had fired. Within a split second, I felt a hot poker sensation in the middle of my right thigh. I looked down and found a large, black circle in my pants leg with a hole in the middle.

"Damn, it burns," I said, grabbing my leg. A wave of nausea doubled me over, and I almost puked. My forehead broke out with beads of sweat, and I was about to pass out.

Freeman had turned white as a ghost. "Did I shoot you?"

"Hell, yes!" I yelled, and collapsed back in the chair.

"Dorris, Dorris, I'm so sorry."

143

Gulley eased me to the floor, and I heard Boraff running to get a medic. I passed out as Gulley wrapped his belt around my thigh. I awoke when they put me on a stretcher and carried me to an aid station. When they gave me morphine before the ninety-mile ambulance trip to a hospital, I passed out again.

When I came to in the hospital, I'd had surgery on my right leg, and it was two days later, May 8. I thanked God that I still had my leg. The man in the bed next to me told me the war was over.

It was over—I couldn't believe it. We drank wine, and several patients smoked cigarettes in celebration. I reached for my clothes, looking for my precious cigarette butt in the tin can. It wasn't there. I'd kept it in the right side pocket of my pants. I had the staff search everywhere for it, but the can was gone. I hated losing that more than being shot.

While praying that night, it dawned on me that losing the cigarette butt would be a greater reminder of what had happened here than if I'd kept it as a memorial. I committed to never forget the beautiful spirit of that severely malnourished human being, the hell that he'd survived at Dachau, and his most precious gift of love, an answer to my prayer.

The next day my surgeon told me that one more inch over and the bullet would have severed my femoral artery, and I'd have bled to death. He'd also found that my right foot was broken. I told him I'd broken it running through a plowed field near Schweinfurt.

On Tuesday, I flew to a general hospital in Rheims, France, where I spent the next two months recovering. The best part of my recovery was that I had access to a beautiful nearby cathedral.

Albert had taken my leg injury very hard even though Dad tried and tried to convince him I was okay. Finally, Mom sent me a letter saying Albert had received my letter in which I'd written I'd be home as soon as I could, and we'd ride bikes for hours every day. It had made all the difference for Albert.

When I returned to my outfit, I got off the truck and Freeman embraced me. Then he pulled up my pants leg and let out a loud cheer.

"You didn't lose your leg! I thought you'd lost it."

"The doctors saved it."

"Dorris, I'm sorry."

"Don't worry about it, kid."

Gulley had sent me a letter saying that some of the other guys were so mad when they heard Freeman shot me that they told him I lost my leg.

Boraff and Gulley approached us with smiles.

"Let's go get some hasenpfeffer," Gulley said. "And Freeman, you're buying."

Heading for that local diner, it felt good to be with my buddies again.

✸ ✸ ✸

We moved on to Salzburg, Austria next. For a couple of weeks, we guarded German prisoners clearing roads, but mostly we just hung out and enjoyed the view—the Alps, the Salzach River, cobblestone streets, the medieval and baroque buildings. Salzburg was an enchanting place.

Next we moved to Linz, Austria, where we guarded a POW camp of about five thousand German prisoners. I worked inside the camp and one of my jobs was to pick up supplies every day. I usually picked one prisoner to help me, and we'd drive a truck into town and bring supplies back to camp. I never had any problems. I was amazed at how disciplined the German soldiers were. It was easy to recognize the prisoners who were hardened with less capacity for empathy and those who were indecent just like Bellum.

I got to know a few decent prisoners and realized they'd been impacted deeply, and most had lost their very selves. Many had marched since they were in grade school to the kettledrum beat of war. There were even a few who had never fallen under Hitler's spell. They'd resisted, maintaining freedom. I made friends with one of them.

A week later on Thursday, I still hadn't figured out why I'd been spared when so many—Gillum, McLaurin, Gilberto, Bloss, Gee, Smith, Jodrey, and others—had paid the ultimate sacrifice. But I'd be going home soon and, hopefully, could figure it out later. Then I thought: *No; I'm still here. There's something I've not done or discovered yet.*

Late that afternoon Kallaher gave us our new orders, my final orders. I had one more assignment before I could go home.

VIENNA

Six weeks later, we'd relocated to Vienna, a city on the blue-green Danube, home of Beethoven and Mozart, and once the cultural center of the world. I stood in a shower enjoying the warm water massaging my back and shoulders, thinking how lucky I was to be alive.

Why had I been spared? What is it I'm supposed to do? Maybe I'm just a lucky soldier.

I turned off the water, grabbed my towel, and dried off. I hurried down the hall and into the bedroom, slipped on my boxers, and headed back to the bathroom.

I wiped the foggy mirror, lathered up, and began shaving, thinking about Vienna. The city had been bombed many times near the end of the war, and there were buildings on every block reduced to remnant walls. Every day on my walk to work, I passed by two cathedrals with steeples still standing but shattered windows and everything inside reduced to rubble. Almost all the civilian vehicles had been destroyed, and most of the trolleys too. The few remaining red-and-white-topped electric trolleys were usually overcrowded, standing room only. I patted my face with Gulley's cologne and rinsed out the sink.

Post-war the city—like Austria—had been divided into four zones, controlled respectively by France, United States, United Kingdom, and Russia. Walking back to my room, I thought about the concrete towers that the Nazis had used. They stood as the only reminder of what had led to the bombing and wrecking of this great town, and what had brought us all together here.

Grabbing my clean uniform from the closet, I dressed quickly, thinking about the opera and all the great things this city had to offer. I'd had several jobs since arriving a month and a half ago. For the last two weeks, I'd guarded German prisoners as they unloaded flour for a company that made Vienna bread—I'd never tasted better warm-buttered bread.

Last night Gulley, Boraff, and I had lapped up a large bag of that delicious bread and talked about how Mingus would've loved V-bread. We all missed him. And after dinner we all played poker till the early hours of the morning and shared embellished battlefield stories about Mingus with Freeman, the kid who'd never met him. Secretly, I was glad Mingus had been sent home. I didn't want him getting killed.

Heading toward the door, I glanced at all the boots in the hardwood foyer. The guys were upstairs playing poker again. Our entire squad lived here in this two-story, yellow stucco row house on a hill in Grinzing—a suburb about five miles northwest of Vienna's center—where trees lined the narrow streets and where coffee shops and cafés had reopened. I sat on the sofa, put on my boots, and then gazed out the front room window. I could see the giant, two-hundred-foot tall Ferris wheel guarding the entrance to an amusement park just north of the city.

It was Friday night, and I needed to get moving. I hurried out alone on my way to the famous Vienna opera. Catching a trolley car, I shouldered my way to the back and stood next to a decorated French soldier with medals and ribbons galore on his chest. I glanced to my right at an older couple dressed for a night on the town, who were sitting close and holding hands, reminding me of the Munich dentist and his wife.

About twenty minutes later, we reached my stop. I followed a small group of people off the trolley and walked up three blocks then down a street to a grand, beige stone opera house with Roman arches and Greek columns. I hustled inside and goggled at beautiful mini arches decorating the mezzanine level. At the front of the enormous music hall, the elevated mahogany stage framed by red velvet curtains ignited my imagination, and I daydreamed about all the greats who'd performed there—Beethoven, Mozart, and Mahler to name a few.

I thanked the usher for the program, found my seat in the last row, and leaned back to take it all in as black, navy, and gray wool suits accompanied blue, white, and yellow dresses with matching felt hats—aristocrats and elegant couples—parading toward their seats. The orchestra tuned their instruments for several minutes and then played the overture of Beethoven's *Fidelio*. I closed my eyes and envisioned a world free from the misery of need, free from war. The music lifted my spirits as if a new day were dawning, rescuing the world from what had just happened.

The performance ran late. When I got out, I raced down two blocks, taking a short cut through a deserted, bombed-out section, hoping to catch a trolley back to Grinzing. The last car for the night was readying to leave, and it was completely loaded. Some people were hanging onto the outside, their arms hooked over open windows. It was impossible for me to get in that car. Unrolling my sleeves in the cool of night, I'd resigned myself for a five-mile walk back to Grinzing when a bearded Russian soldier in the trolley car gazing through a window at me, stood at attention as if he was going to salute me. Instead he took the machine gun from his shoulder and let off a burst of fire, rattling bullets through the top of the trolley.

People screamed in panic and jumped off the car, fleeing in all directions, some running around me. I remained perfectly still, intrigued by the Russian with red patches on both shoulders and red badges on his collar. Within seconds, the car was empty. He came to the door, bowed, and held out his arm in a gesture to welcome me aboard.

I was in uniform but not on duty, so I wasn't carrying a weapon. A little apprehensive but more curious, I stepped up and cautiously entered the car, taking a seat across from the robust, black-bearded Russian, who ordered the conductor to move out.

"You're American," he said with a raspy baritone voice.

"Yes. You're Russian. Thank you for—"

"No worry, comrade. Those Nazi-lovers deserve to walk. To be killed. They are guilty too. They stood by and did nothing."

The silence that followed grew uncomfortable.

"They're human beings, not soldiers," I said. "What could they have done?"

"They're all collectively just as guilty as Hitler and Himmler."

"No," I said, shaking my head. "I don't believe in collective guilt, unearned guilt. They didn't—"

"They didn't try to stop it," the Russian interrupted in an agitated tone then asked, "Where did you serve?"

"I'm a Rainbow Division soldier," I said, glancing at the rainbow patch on my shoulder. "We liberated many towns, including Dachau."

"Ahh, yes. So you know what the Nazis did. I saw with my own eyes what they'd done at Warsaw and Auschwitz." The Russian paused. "You and I know."

I cringed just thinking about the atrocities I'd seen.

"Dachau ..." My voice cracked as the emotion welled

up. I looked down, biting the inside of my cheek, not wanting to cry. "They gassed the elderly, the weak, and the young; some of them had been mowed down by machine guns, falling in and around the railroad cars and others in mass graves. Many had died buried alive in boxcars, suffocating to death on that train ride to hell." I raised my head and looked at the Russian. "The Nazis starved the others till they were walking skeletons. They deprived them of being human. They starved them of love."

The Russian sat back against the seat and arched his brow with a questioning expression. "I heard about American reprisals at Dachau. You're in Roosevelt's SS division?"

"No, no!" I said. "I serve as a soldier in the US Army's Forty-Second Infantry Division."

I didn't want to talk about the reprisals, reflex reactions to the emotional outrage that any human being could have committed in that moment of discovery, seeing those well-fed SS guards responsible for thousands of starved and dead bodies, surrendering and begging for our mercy.

The Russian flitted a smile as if he understood, and then a tear rolled down his cheek. "I was in the Sixtieth Russian Army," he said, and paused for several seconds. "I lost five brothers: Vladimir in the Prague offensive…Joseph at Krakow…Alexander in Warsaw…Dimitri and Fyodor, my youngest brothers, were killed by eight-year-old German boys firing an antiaircraft weapon in Berlin."

I gaped in shock and sadness. "I'm so sorry for your losses. I'm so sorry."

The Russian looked away as if he might break down. I wanted to console him but didn't know what to say.

"We lost some great men," I said. "They were like brothers to me. I loved them all. I'll never forget them."

The Russian met my gaze, his eyes filled with indignation. He lowered his voice. "The Nazis are still out there; they'll morph and adjust. They'll become a new species, a

more efficient Nazi, creating their own international enter-
prise, giving themselves license to control, to work, to abuse,
and to treat people like animals again. They'll find a way. We
must kill them all!"

The trolley slowed as it approached the Grinzing Village
stop.

"This is my stop," I said, alerting the conductor. I turned
and peered into the Russian's dark eyes. "There's been enough
killing. Enough!"

"American fool!" he said, raising his voice. "You're going
to get off this car, and all your struggle will have been for
nothing. No purpose."

My heart pounded. Then a wave of warmth and joy illuminated my mind. I rose to my feet, grinned, and slowly shook
my head. "No. I'm going to get off this trolley and find the
love of my life and have lots of babies. I'm going to love them
and help them direct their attention to channel love and goodness into the world. Then they'll have babies and teach their
babies to channel goodness and love into the world."

The Russian's eyes twinkled, and then he smiled. "You're
Catholic."

"Yes," I said, and produced a big smile thinking about
my childhood neighbors, Billy and Tommy Daniels.

"*Udachi!*"

"What does that mean?"

The Russian continued smiling. "Good luck, comrade.
Good luck."

I moved my heels together, stood at attention for a long
moment, saluted him, did an about-face, and strode off the
trolley with the wind at my back, knowing everything I'd been
through had prepared me for tonight.

Reflecting on the long journey from Camp Gruber to
Dachau and then to Vienna, ending in the trolley ride with a
Russian, I walked slowly for a couple of blocks, looking down
at the street, deep in thought, then stopped, looked up at

the stars, and prayed in gratitude. I found Polaris, the North Star, and many other stars emerged beyond. My entire body warmed and tingled from my head to my toes as if the ecstasy of infinity had washed over me. I stretched my right arm toward the heavens, wanting to touch the hand of God.

I'd discovered my meaning.

EPILOGUE

Jim Dorris found the love of his life, Charlotte Marie Snow, and they married in Rochester, New York, in 1949. Before going to bed on their honeymoon night, they knelt beside the bed, held hands, and prayed—a practice they enjoyed for the next sixty-six years. They raised five loving boys and two loving girls who produced ten grandsons and eight granddaughters, all channels for love and goodness to come into the world.

On April 14, 2019, I met with Jim, and we went over the last scene of the story. After our meeting, as we made our way toward the door, I stopped, turned, shook his hand with tears in my eyes, and told him I loved him. Jim smiled, holding my hand an extra couple of seconds, his eyes glistening with meaning and love.

Sadly, four days later on April 18, Jim departed this world. He'd reached the hand of God and now dwells in the presence of goodness.

AFTERWORD

Private James F. Dorris and Dr. Viktor E. Frankl searched for meaning on eerily similar journeys despite their different circumstances and the different questions life asked of them. Dorris, a twenty-year-old, green American soldier drafted into war, found and fulfilled his true essence meaning after liberating the inmates at Dachau. Frankl was a thirty-nine-year-old accomplished neurologist and psychiatrist from Vienna and prisoner at Auschwitz where he found, and later after liberation, fulfilled his true essence meaning—helping others find their meaning. Their parallel journeys resonate in history and point to our future.

A Soldier's Search provides the missing piece of the human-meaning puzzle, complementing Frankl's life and work. The liberating soldier's journey completes the search. The thematic plot of humankind, our grand purpose has been uncovered.

Dorris and Frankl's searches, carried out under extreme conditions, reveal a common theme about freedom and God as they both achieved the highest meaning humans could obtain under their respective circumstances.

Their separate achievements lead to the inevitable conclusion. If you follow the will for meaning of individual humans into the future toward infinity, their true essence meanings will become one. First their meanings will merge into an odyssey for freedom: freedom from slavery, from tyranny, from the misery of need, and from the bondage of time—freedoms inconceivable and unachievable without internal freedom underpinned by the phenomenology of God. Then the grand purpose of life will culminate when humans approach the ecstasy of infinity, where we'll reach out, touch the hand of God, and dwell in the radiance of goodness.

ABOUT THE AUTHORS

JAMES F. DORRIS achieved his true essence meaning and has inspired many with his exemplary life of love and his pursuit of God. Several years after the war, Rainbow troops and survivors of Dachau reunited. James befriended and maintained lifelong contact with several of those he'd helped liberate. He never forgot his fellow soldiers, Dachau, the orphans, the little girl who lost her Papa, or the other horrors of war, keeping them in perspective. He claimed he never would have survived without the goodness of God.

For his service in World War II, he was awarded a Purple Heart, Bronze Star, a combat infantry badge, and four campaign ribbons. In 2001 the 222nd Regiment was awarded the Presidential Unit Citation for courageous action, taking a relentless artillery onslaught and stopping the last major German offensive on January 24–25, 1945.

James believed the inch-long cigarette butt earned at Dachau was the greatest award of his life.

JC HOWELL MD is an author who writes about love, freedom, meaning, and God. For more see:
http://www.authorjchowell.com

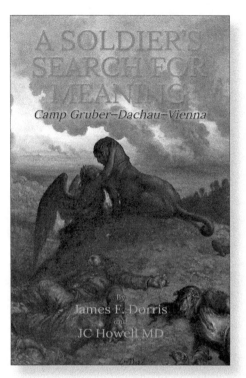

A Soldier's Search for Meaning
Camp Gruber—Dachau—Vienna
James F. Dorris and JC Howell MD

Author website: authorjchowell.com
Publisher: SDP Publishing
Also available in ebook format

Also by JC Howell MD
Sentio
Strange Love in America

 **SDP Publishing**

www.SDPPublishing.com
Contact us at: info@SDPPublishing.com

9 781733 821469